THE PSYCHOLOGICAL METHODS OF TESTING INTELLIGENCE

Educational Psychology Monographs
Edited by Guy Montrose Whipple

No. 13

THE PSYCHOLOGICAL METHODS OF TESTING INTELLIGENCE

By

WILLIAM STERN

TRANSLATED FROM THE GERMAN

By

GUY MONTROSE WHIPPLE
Assistant Professor of Educational Psychology, Cornell University.

GYAN

Published by

GYAN

Gyan Publishing House
5, Ansari Road
Daryaganj, New Delhi-110002
Phone: 011-47034999, 9811692060
E-mail: books@gyanbooks.com

Distribution Network
gyanbooks.com
India, USA, Canada, UK, Australia, France

ISBN : 978-81-212-6246-0 (PB)
First Published, 1914

2nd Impression 2022

Printed at: Gyan Press, Delhi.

THE PSYCHOLOGICAL METHODS OF TESTING INTELLIGENCE
Author: WILLIAM STERN

Educational Psychology Monographs

Edited by Guy Montrose Whipple

No. 13

THE PSYCHOLOGICAL METHODS OF TESTING INTELLIGENCE

By

WILLIAM STERN

TRANSLATED FROM THE GERMAN
BY

GUY MONTROSE WHIPPLE

Assistant Professor of Educational Psychology
Cornell University.

1914

CONTENTS

AUTHOR'S PREFACE

I undertook for the last German congress of psychology, held at Berlin, April, 1912, a general review of the psychological methods of testing intelligence. As I had only an hour at my disposal in my address, I could at that time do little more than outline certain of the main features of this very broad field. It seemed to me, however, hardly desirable to publish the address in the form in which it was given. I felt, on the contrary, that in view of the now ever-increasing interest displayed in the theme both in Germany and elsewhere and in view of the extraordinarily scattered nature of the literature—much of which, by the way, is difficult of access—that an exposition of the topic on a wider scale was demanded. So I have tried to elaborate my original review to this larger scale. I have treated in it three main topics: single tests, the serial method (after Binet-Simon) and the methods of correlation and estimation.

In the form of my treatment, also, I have overstepped the bounds of the mere "general review." I have not confined myself to setting down what now exists, but have myself taken an attitude toward the problem, have offered criticisms of the methods and made proposals for their modification and development. In making these criticisms and suggestions I have been able to use the experience that has come from the tests of intelligence which have been in progress at Breslau for some years past. Many of these experiments, in which psychologists, educators and physicians have coöperated in a gratifying manner, have already been published; others are still in progress. Yet, thanks to the courtesy of these workers, I am able to make a preliminary report of some of these as yet unfinished investigations. I have also taken the opportunity to incorporate some minor contributions to the problem that have originated in the exercises of the Psychological Seminary at Breslau.

The subject under discussion is limited to some extent by the circumstance that tests of intelligence have been almost always restricted to children and youths. But it is just the peculiarity of the psychological methods of intelligence testing—psychological in the narrower sense, in contrast, *e. g.*, to the psychiatrical methods—that they take their start from the mental life of the child, though later, of course, the attempt is made to carry them over into test methods for adults. On this account I have treated in some detail the results that accrue to pedagogy, and not only to the pedagogy of auxiliary classes and of the subnormal child, but also to the pedagogy of the normal child.

In my judgment, intelligence testing is one of the most promising fields of *applied* psychology, using that term in the strictest sense. For this reason I wanted to make this survey of it accessible to wider circles of readers outside the psychological profession, especially to teachers of normal and of backward children, to school administrative authorities, to school physicians, to specialists in nervous and in children's diseases, and to those engaged in child welfare work. This special edition, accordingly, has been arranged. I hope that it will demonstrate to the workers in these circles the great importance and fruitfulness of the psychologist's methods and at the same time show them the difficulties and the gaps in the present status of this work, and that so plainly as to prevent overhasty attempts at practical application.

W. Stern.

Breslau, October, 1912.

TRANSLATOR'S PREFACE

This translation of Stern's *Die psychologischen Methoden der Intelligenzprüfung* has been undertaken because the monograph, though dealing with a different topic, aims, like my previous translation of Offner's *Mental Fatigue,* to collate, systematize and appraise a mass of scattered and to most readers inaccessible material that bears upon a problem of unquestioned importance.

Professor Stern was one of the pioneers and most active expositors of the investigation of the psychology of testimony, for the furtherance of which he instituted a new periodical, *Beiträge zur Psychologie der Aussage,* which was later enlarged to cover the wider field of applied psychology in general (*Zeitschrift für angewandte Psychologie*). Stern is likewise well-known for his contributions to individual psychology, notably for his important work on individual differences (*Ueber Psychologie der individuellen Differenzen*), published originally in 1900 and completely rewritten in 1911 under the title, *Die differentielle Psychologie,* and for his numerous significant contributions to the psychology of childhood. From his Psychological Seminary at Breslau have appeared many researches, some of which are reported for the first time in the present monograph. In conjunction with Lipmann he has also founded the *Institut für angewandte Psychologie,* which aims to serve as a museum and clearing house for the collection and dissemination of methods and materials for studying and recording the mental processes of individuals and for facilitating the application of psychology to various practical problems.

What Stern has aimed to do in the present monograph is sufficiently set forth in his own preface, but it may be added here that his book affords what is, so far as I know, the best, and in fact almost the only authoritative, critical and compact general survey of the literature of intelligence testing which is adapted for lay readers as well as for professional psychologists.

In perfecting this translation I have received much valuable aid from the members of my class in German Educational Psychology, in which the monograph was used as a text, and from my colleagues, Professor P. R. Pope, of the German Department, and Mr. D. K. Fraser, assistant in Educational Psychology.

GUY MONTROSE WHIPPLE.

Cornell University, January 1st, 1914.

THE PSYCHOLOGICAL METHODS OF TESTING INTELLIGENCE

INTRODUCTION

Nature and Problem of Intelligence Testing

1. *Intelligence and Intelligence Testing*

Modern experimental psychology, which started with the study of sense-perception and then undertook that of ideas and feelings, has in the last decade begun to deal with intellectual functions themselves. And it is worthy of note that general theoretical psychology and differential applied psychology took this step forward at the same time, though for the most part independently. In the former there was developed a psychology of thinking, in the latter there appeared the investigation of differences in intelligence.

Our discussion must be restricted to the second problem with which alone we are concerned. To the other branch of psychology we may confidently leave the question of the general nature of intellectual activity and the investigation of the phenomena that constitute thinking as such. What we are interested in is not intelligence as a phenomenon, but intelligence as a capacity and particularly a capacity with respect to which men differ one from another. And intelligence testing is the determination of the degree of this capacity in a given individual.

The objection is often made that the problem of intellectual diagnosis can in no way be successfully dealt with until we have exact knowledge of the general nature of intelligence itself. But this objection does not seem to me pertinent. In science there is no such precise sequence of the different research problems. We measure electro-motive force without knowing what electricity is, and we diagnose with very delicate test methods many diseases the real nature of which we know as yet very little. Indeed, it may be asserted, quite on the contrary, that progress in testing intelligence may shed light from a new angle upon the theoretical study of intelligence and thus supplement the psychology of thinking in a valuable manner. If it turns out, for instance, that certain symptoms are relevant and others irrelevant for the differentiation of the intelligence shown by different persons; if, again, one series of these symptoms exhibit a high degree, another series a less degree of intercorrelation, then our knowledge of the structure of intelligence must thereby be little by little increased, and thus there will develop a fruitful reciprocity between the two phases of investigation, theoretical and applied.

Naturally, we cannot begin our work without a preliminary definition of intelligence, however provisional it may be. And this definition must be neither too broad nor too narrow.

Many psychiatrists have used a definition of intelligence that is too broad. They use intelligence, in fact, to include mental attainments of all kinds, all those mental qualities, then, that are not volitional or emotional. If this position be taken, it follows, evidently that the examination of immediate memory, of ability to learn, of range of information, of fidelity of report, or of discriminative sensitivity is just as much a constituent part of intelligence testing as the examination of ability to apprehend, to synthetize, of capacity to judge, to conclude, to define, to criticize, etc. Again, a question that is very important for us, viz.: to what extent intelligence really enters into these first-named activities, and whether and in what way it shows signs of its presence in them, becomes absurd. But the advance made in the recent development of intelligence testing, in contrast to the uncritical determination of mental level by any sort of questions and tests, consists in the fact that we not only limit intelligence by setting it over against the emotive and volitional nature of an individual, but also ascribe to it a definitely restricted place within the mental functions.

This delimitation of the sphere of intelligence that is even now essential cannot be effected, in my opinion, from a phenomenological. but only from a teleological point of view. In fact, my definition is this: *Intelligence is a general capacity of an individual consciously to adjust his thinking to new requirements: it is general mental adaptability to new problems and conditions of life.*

This definition differentiates intelligence clearly from other mental capacities.

The fact that the adjustment is made to the *new* distinguishes intelligence from *memory* whose fundamental teleological feature is the conservation and utilization of conscious contents already given.

The fact of *adaptation*, again, emphasizes the dependence of the performances upon external factors, on the problems and demands of life, and thus distinguishes intelligence from *genius,* whose nature is to create the new spontaneously.

Finally, the fact that the capacity is a *general capacity* distinguishes intelligence from *talent* the characteristic of which is precisely the limitation of efficiency to one kind of content. He is intelligent, on the contrary, who is able easily to effect mental adaptation to new requirements under the most varied conditions and in the most varied fields. If talent be a material efficiency, intelligence is a formal efficiency.

I trust that these distinctions may serve to lessen the confusion that has been current. It is not so long ago, indeed, that in psychiatry 'information tests' were carried on as 'intelligence tests,' thereby confusing memory and intelligence. And we often, even nowadays, find intelligence and talent confused in everyday life. In the school, for instance, a teacher of a special subject like mathematics, who perceives the special gift of a pupil in that field, may easily come to believe without further evidence that this pupil has general ability, or in other words, to rate him as an intelligent pupil.

But we should not interpret this delimitation to mean the erection of sharply distinct faculties, as in the old faculty theory. Intelligence, for instance, does not function by itself and memory by itself; rather, every operation of memory is more or less impregnated with intellectual functions and *vice versa:* the extent of this interconnection can be indicated only by the correlation of the tested symptoms.

But just on account of this composite character of every actual mental process it seems to me that the definition of intelligence I have given above is indispensable as a regulative principle for further investigation: I mean that any sort of perceptive, memorial or attentive activity is at the same time an intelligent activity *just in so far as it includes a new adjustment to new demands.*

We must add one final limitation: we are considering only those phases of intelligence testing that deal with a *scale of degrees.* This does not mean to minimize in the slightest the importance of qualitative differences in types of intelligence (analytic-synthetic, objective-subjective, etc.); we need only refer to the importance of the essay as a means of testing for these phases.[1] But we shall discuss in this monograph only those forms of procedure that permit us to say of a given person that his intelligence is of such and such degree.

As the title of the book indicates, the problem of method will be prominent throughout our presentation. We can thus best do justice to the present status of the question, for the significance of the results thus far obtained lies particularly in the fact that they serve to provide new suggestions for the perfecting of our methods.

2. *Practical Problems of Intelligence Testing*

Since we have to do here not with methods designed for purely theoretical investigations, but with

[1]On this aspect of intelligence, consult the general review and bibliography given in my earlier discussion (1: pp. 203-213, 433-4).

[Note: numbers in parentheses refer, unless otherwise indicated, to the reference list at the end of this monograph.—*Translator.*]

methods that are to be employed in daily life, their form is determined, at least in part, by the practical needs that are to be satisfied by intelligence testing. We must distinguish four groups that arise from the combination of the two pairs of terms: abnormal and normal, adult and child.[2]

(*a*) *Adult, abnormal individuals* form the chief material of the psychiatrists, who in consequence were the first to want to test intelligence.[3] Not only have they invented single methods, but they have also devised whole series or systems of examination (Rieger, Kraepelin, Sommer, Ziehen; Gregor, Bernstein, Rossolimo, *et al.*) The contents of these systems are such as to bring them only partially within our scope; by far the greater portion of them take on the character of questions and qualitative tests rather than that of quantitatively gradable tests; even where these latter have been used, comparative material for normal persons is often enough wanting. Whether the outcome of any one of these tests might really indicate an abnormally weak intelligence was frequently judged on the basis of a preconceived opinion as to how normal men might be expected to react to the test in question. In recent years this has been remedied. Rodenwald (22) showed with regard to a group of information tests how much of what had *a priori* been deemed abnormal really lay within the bounds of normality. Many psychiatrists have sought to obtain comparative standards for

[2] A similar division is used by Meumann (15), though he, to be sure, defines intelligence somewhat more broadly than do we.

[3] An extensive general summary of the more important methods of intelligence testing used by alienists will be found in Jaspers (12).

their methods by extensive application of them to normal persons (Sommer, 26; Ziehen, 30; Ranschburg; Rossolimo, 23-25). Others have turned to account the fact that certain methods had already been tried out extensively by psychologists upon normal persons, *e. g.*, Ebbinghaus' completion method, the report experiment.[4] But how far all this comes from meeting the need of the alienist himself is shown by the decision of the International Congress of Physicians to turn to the psychologists in order to secure normal series for the various psychiatrical tests of intelligence. This task has been undertaken by the Institute for Applied Psychology.

(*b*) *Abnormal children* have become, just in the last few decades, a center of pedagogical, socio-political, and medical interest. The whole pedagogy of the subnormal, the schema of auxiliary schools and special classes, the juvenile court and the various protective and corrective institutions are, indeed, matters of very recent development, but they are demanding a more exact study of the individuality of the child, both for purposes of mental diagnosis and for 'psychotechnic' purposes (training, treatment, punishment, etc.). To meet these needs, the determination of degree of intelligence is, though not the only, at least a most important factor.

The weaknesses of the psychiatrical methods mentioned above were doubled when these methods were applied to these new problems. With adults we knew little enough of the normal standard to which the performances of abnormal subjects were to be com-

---

[4] For a general account of these methods, see the translator's *Manual of Mental and Physical Tests*, Baltimore, 2d ed., 1914.

pared, but with children we knew nothing at all. What is more, one normal standard is not enough in this case; every age-year must have its own standard. The magnitude of a defect of intelligence in a nine-year old child can be determined only by comparing it with the normal nine-year old intelligence, and so with other ages. The consequent demand for the creation of normal test-series for each year of childhood was met, as a matter of fact, not from the side of psychiatry, but from that of psychology. Alfred Binet, with the coöperation of the physician, Simon, has created such a graded series of tests; and although the system as it now stands may be far from final, its fundamental conception will retain its permanent value and will doubtless lead us ultimately to a completely satisfactory solution. His method has already attained international usage. We shall discuss it fully in the second part of our treatment.

(*c*) *Normal children and youths.* It is not to be supposed, however, that intelligence testing of normal children has merely the secondary importance of supplying standards of comparison for investigations of the feeble-minded. On the contrary, the gradation of intelligence within the range of normality is an entirely independent problem that is closely connected with practical pedagogical interests. The ordinary school examinations afford a notion of the pupil's knowledge and of his external accomplishments, but they do not afford an index of his inner endowment, of his mental maturity and power; it is here that psychological tests must supplement other forms of examination. This need is especially evident at entrance examinations, but it exists within the ordinary administration of the school as well, for the demand, nowadays so emphatically voiced, that instruction shall be individualized to the fullest possible extent, presupposes a fuller insight into the nature of individualities. Very recently, in fact, serious attempts have been made to make divisions into classes and sections on a psychological and qualitative basis (special classes for the subnormal, classes for the backward, separate classes for the specially gifted, 'parallel' classes with normal and minimal courses of instruction for pupils of different degrees of ability in particular subjects)—attempts that demand, as an indispensable prerequisite the possibility of very exact determination of the actual degree of mental ability.[5]

In this connection we must, of course, guard against the danger which is apt to arise of supposing that we have grasped the individuality of a pupil in its totality when we have tested his intelligence. The fact that intelligence can be more easily treated quantitatively than can other individual capacities must not lead us to overestimate its import. Nevertheless, the fact that we can deal with intelligence by itself does serve to disclose the structure of the individuality. We can determine whether a perform-

[5]All these pedagogical reform-movements that are related to the problem of intelligence were the general subject of discussion at the first German Congress for Child Training and Paidology (*Kongress für Jugendbildung und Jugendkunde*) that it was conducted by the School Reform Association (*Bund für Schulreform*) at Dresden, 1911. The addresses and discussions of this congress have been published in separate form (11): the special problem of testing intelligence was discussed in the addresses of Meumann, Kramer, and the author.

ance of greater or lesser degree depends on talent or on intelligence; we can investigate what degree of correspondence exists between the experimental results and the teachers' judgments of the intelligence of pupils; we can delimit the extent to which general school efficiency is dependent on intelligence itself on the one hand and on non-intellectual factors on the other hand—a delimitation that, as will be shown later, forms one of the chief merits of the psychological methods.

The studies of normal children that bear directly upon our problem were first carried on by *separate tests:* this method, originated in Germany, has been very extensively employed and further developed in France and especially in America. Then arose in France *Binet's system of tests with age gradations* that we have already mentioned. England has lately joined the movement to good effect by giving us the *correlation method* for use in the more precise testing of intelligence (Pearson, Spearman, *et al.*) These three main lines of activity will furnish the principle of division of our subsequent treatment.

(*d*) *Normal adults.* Here we find ourselves in a realm whose exploitation is entirely in the future, for the tests of intelligence thus far administered to normal adults have not been undertaken for the sake of these persons, but only to get comparative standards for abnormal persons. Yet even now new developments are to be noted. Münsterberg shows how important an exact knowledge of individuality would be for determining choice of a vocation and he has already suggested ways in which the vocational bureaus that exist in America might arrange psychological tests (19, 20). And Captain Meyer (17, 18) sees in intelligence testing a method that ought to help the recruiting office to keep unfit candidates off the enlistment rolls.

These last considerations show that the chief emphasis of intelligence testing, which has hitherto lain wholly within psychopathology, must in the future be shifted distinctly toward normal psychology: so the labor expended by psychology in securing a reliable method will benefit not only physicians and those concerned in teaching the abnormal, but also jurists, military officials, those concerned in teaching the normal child and others.

But just this anticipated extension of the practical applicability of intelligence tests necessitates several words of warning.

(*a*) We are still in the midst of our *preliminary work* on method. The methods that now prevail—and this is true also of the Binet-Simon system—are not yet to be regarded as diagnostic canons that admit of official prescription. The law passed in New Jersey that directs the use of intelligence tests with all pupils suspected of backwardness seems on this account very premature. So, too, it will be long, very long, before we realize the optimistic hope that Spearman attaches to the correlation method of testing intelligence, when he says: "Indeed, it seems possible to foresee the day when there will be an annual official determination of the 'intellectual index' of every child in the empire" (Hart-Spearman; 75, p. 78).

(*b*) It must be understood that tests of intelligence are not easy to conduct. Their administration demands extended practise, psychological training, and a critical mind. Thus, for instance, the average teacher, whose work has been with the wholly different methods of pedagogical questioning and examining, is very apt to apply psychological tests in those forms in which their value would be positively illusory. If, accordingly, the use of tests for practical purposes shall attain any very large currency, the training of a specially psychologically drilled personnel will become a necessity. School psychologists would then take their place side by side with the school physicians.[6]

What erroneous ideas prevail concerning the ease of conducting tests is illustrated, *e. g.*, in the declaration of Captain Meyer that in military enlistment tests of intelligence could some day be carried on quite mechanically by subalterns. But, as a matter of fact, a psychological test is quite a different thing than the determination of weight or of stature which might very well be carried out by minor military officers.

(*c*) Psychological tests *must not be overestimated,* as if they were complete and automatically operative measures of mind. At most they are the psychographic minimum that gives us a first orientation concerning individuals about whom nothing else is known, and they are of service to complement and to render comparable and objectively gradable other observations—psychological, pedagogical, medical—not to replace these.[7]

---

[7]Similar warnings against the overestimation, mechanization and diletante employment of tests are to be found in Myers (21), Bobertag (40), and also in Binet's last work (37, pp. 155 ff.).

[Cf. also the translator's *Manual of Mental and Physical Tests,* Ch. 1.]

[6]On the demand for school psychologists, see 11, p. 19.

[The situation in America is discussed by J. E. W. Wallin in two interesting papers, *Jour. of Educ. Psychol.* 2: 1911, 121 and 191.—*Translator.*]

I. Single Tests and Series of Tests

1. *Single Tests*

All psychological experiments may be divided, according to their problem, into research experiments and test experiments. The latter are now generally known as "tests;" their aim is "to determine for a given individual his mental constitution or personality or to determine a single one of his mental traits.[1]" Tests include, of course, not only experiments in the narrower meaning of an investigation carried out with the aid of instruments, but also simple methods of procedure that do not involve the use of instruments—questions, problems, presentation of pictures, and the like—provided that these are administered in a systematic and scientifically regulated manner and that their results are recorded.

Now, in no field have so many tests been proposed and put into operation as in the field of intelligence testing. To give a complete exposition of all these test methods and of the results that have been gained through them would exceed the bounds of this monograph. But this is not necessary, after all, because, as will be shown in a moment, the fundamental significance of our whole problem lies not in

[1]See my earlier text (1, p. 87).

the single tests, but in the construction of well-considered systems of tests, for which single tests merely supply the raw material. So we shall content ourselves in this part of our essay with a cursory survey without any pretense at all to completeness.[2]

The varied nature of the proposals and test investigations thus far made is due to the fact that the same problem has been approached in very different ways.

(*a*) For a long time we started from the erroneous presupposition that any psychological method of experimentation would be really usable as a test. It was thought that all that was necessary was to alter the direction, so to speak, of the plan of investigation. When a large number of measurements had been secured by a single method on a few persons in the laboratory, the same method was applied to many persons, but only once or a few times to each of them. If it turned out from such a mass experiment that the more intelligent persons obtained, all things considered, better average scores

[2]For all the literature on single tests, see my text on differential psychology (1, 426 ff.); also in Appendix II of that book there is a survey of the relation of the single tests to school performance. Fifty-four different tests, with numerous sub-types are described, together with their methods and chief results, in Whipple's *Manual* (28). A very large collection of materials for testing was exhibited by the Institute for Applied Psychology at the Berlin Congress, Easter, 1912, for information about which Lipmann's catalog in the report of the Congress may be consulted. Since the meeting, this exhibit has been made a permanent one and has been assigned a room in the exhibition by the Prussian Ministry of Education of German material for instruction, at Berlin, 126 Friedrichstrasse. The exhibit can be seen at that place by previous appointment with the Secretary of the Institute (Dr. Lipmann, Telephone Potsdam, No. 8).

than the less intelligent, then it was assumed that the method would answer for testing intelligence.

Nearly all the methods that were familiar to the psychological experimenter have been tested out in this way, especially in the earlier periods of investigation by mental tests, *e. g.*, measurements of reaction-time, determinations of the threshold of differential sensitivity in the different modalities, optical illusions, experiments on motor skill or strength, association experiments, tachistoscopic experiments, learning of syllables, etc. In some cases, it is true, numerous results of interest were secured, but it must be admitted that a good deal of energy has been expended to little avail in these experiments.

(*b*) A significant advance was made when it was finally recognized that this blind probing about could not lead us farther, that, on the contrary, tests of intelligence must be definitely selected on the basis of certain presuppositions that were to be made concerning the nature of intelligence. Investigators, therefore, sought then for exact methods of experimentation that would bring intelligence into direct and manifest operation. To be sure, the problem was at first conceived of in a still too simple form, in that intelligence was thought to be exhibited as a definite clean-cut mental phenomenon and the plan of testing was directed to the examination of this assumed special phenomenon.

The best-known instance of this is the so-called 'combination method' of Ebbinghaus, now better designated as the 'completion method' (5). In Ebbinghaus' view, every true instance of intellectual ability may be reduced in the last analysis to an act of 'combining' *i. e.,* to a process of synthetizing conscious contents that previously had been present separately; accordingly, he invented that method in which the subject of the test is to supply the correct connections between the separated parts of a text in which gaps have been introduced.

This principle of combination or completion has been used by many other investigators as a basis for various forms of test.

Thus, Ries (78) used two tests to measure the ability to bring two terms into a logical relation: A: Pairs of words were presented that had a logical connection, *e. g.,* fire-smoke, flood-need; then a test was made whether the naming of the first member of the pair reinstated the second by dint of the logical connection. B. Single words were given to which such words were to be adjoined as would form a causally connected pair. A similar method is that of Winteler in which a term is to be named that is superordinate, sub-ordinate or co-ordinate to the word given.

The combination test of Masselon in which a meaningful sentence is to be made from three given words has been extensively used. Recently, Meumann (16) has elaborated this method in a special fashion; he presents words so chosen that they can be joined in a sentence either in a banal and logically rather crude way or in a logically pertinent way, *e. g., ass, blows;* poor solution "The ass receives blows." Good solution "The lazy ass receives blows." The tendency toward the former or the latter rendition is taken as an index of intelligence.

Heilbronner's picture-test (8, 27) examines ability to complete in the sphere of vision: the outline of an object is shown on a series of small cards and in such a way that there is a progressive development from an initial very fragmentary outline by successively more detailed stages up to a complete picture of the object. The idea is to find out at what stage of incomplete delineation the object can be recognized.

To this class of tests belongs also the fitting together of cut up pictures (method of the Russian alienists, Bernstein and Rossolimo).

Other psychologists, however, have considered other and quite different mental functions to be the touch-stone of intelligence.

Thus, in an earlier stage of his work Binet (2) believed that the essence of intelligence was capacity to adjust attention: for this reason he used tests of attention, like the cancellation of letters in a specified text (the Bourdon test), the copying of sentences, the esthesiometer (Binet regarded the discrimination of two near-lying compass-points as a phenomenon of attention, not of sensation), the sorting of cards containing the alphabet, or numbers, etc. In the work of Meumann (14) we note at times the laying of a certain one-sided emphasis on the understanding of the abstract as being the root of intelligence. This was why he specially recommended the use in testing of the retention of abstract words. Quite a number of investigators have directed their attention particularly to capacity to apprehend as the index of intelligence, and hence have preferred to use for tests such things as the apprehension of pictures or ability to perceive linguistic material of different contents and extents.

(*c*) We may consider as a third main class of tests those patterned after familiar *pedagogical* tasks. There are, indeed, certain school activities that admit of relatively precise grading, since they can be rated both in terms of quantity (amount done within a given time) and in terms of quality (frequency of mistakes). Those schoolroom tasks are most obviously adaptable for psychological purposes within which the course of activity is fairly homogeneous, *e. g.*, the computation of specified arithmetical problems, writing from dictation, committing to memory of vocabularies and poems, and all these tasks have, in fact, been used for testing intelligence. Evidently a chief objection to this method is that the activities mentioned are dependent to a large degree upon external conditions of the instruction, so that the intelligence of individuals that are working, or that have worked, under different school conditions cannot be subjected to comparative tests by means of these activities.

(*d*) A fourth main class of tests is still farther removed from the precision of the laboratory experiment, but is thereby more nearly allied to real life. These tests aim to secure records of such evidences of intelligence as are accepted in ordinary life as special evidence of it. These direct *tests of intellect* have been specially developed by the psychiatrists: they comprise such things as defining, comparing, differentiating, the understanding of proverbs, grasping the point of a joke, seeing absurdities in verbal or pictorial presentations.

These tests have the advantage that in them intelligence is undoubtedly much more directly operative than in the others: but on this account it is impossible in most of them to scale the results: they are "alternative tests," that admit of but the rough differentiation into right or wrong (+ or —). The single test of this sort, therefore, does not make it possible to secure any very precise characterization of the person tested, or to rank him in a scale.

2. *The Inadequacy of the Single Test*

A critique of all these confusingly many attempts might be undertaken by examining them, test by test, to see which ones deserve to be recommended as indicators of intelligence. But we feel that far more important than such a special scrutiny of single tests is the laying of emphasis upon a general critical position: *no single test, no matter how good it may be, should ever be made the instrument for testing the intelligence of an individual.*[3]

Because the single test tests on the one hand more, and on the other hand, less than it really ought to test.

More, because the mental activity that is aroused in a subject by an experimental task, a test-question, or the like, is the fused resultant of quite varied antecedent conditioning factors: and we do not know what share that particular conditioning factor that we call intelligence played in the performance. In this equivocal nature of the object under investigation lies the too often little noted distinction between tests and laboratory experiments. If I arrange an investigation of memory in the laboratory, I know that I am actually examining memory and not something else, because in numerous single experiments I vary in a measurable way certain conditions only of the function of memory while I keep all the other conditions constant. But when, on the contrary, I administer a test of learning or a test of immediate memory by itself to a person, the outcome is affected by the real capacity of retention, understanding of the material, attention, interest, etc., all without control—and this quite regardless of the disposition of the subject at the time. Or, take another exam-

---

[3]Cf. Binet (36, p. 201): "One test has no meaning, but five or six tests do mean something. * * * The attention of psychologists must, then, be called especially to this principle of the multiplicity of tests."

ple: suppose that a subject has made a good record in the filling out of gaps in a text (Ebbinghaus' completion test), does this good performance depend predominantly upon a real capacity for logical combination? Or upon a specially large vocabulary? Or upon a fine feeling for language? Or upon practise in guessing riddles?

The only way to analyze out from this fused resultant the ability we are after—in this case, for instance, the ability to effect combinations—is obviously to add several more tests of a different kind that will also involve the process of combining, but that will in addition involve mental processes of quite different sorts. Correspondences that may appear in the results of these different tests may then be ascribed with probability to their common factor—in our example, to the ability to effect combinations. The ability sought for must, therefore, be plotted, as it were, from different positions.

Too little. But suppose that we have succeeded in determining a subject's ability to make combinations not by a single test but by a smaller number of different 'combination' tests, have we then measured his intelligence? By no means, for we have now determined far *too little.* Intelligence, it is to be noted, means an all-round ability; it refers to the general mental attitude toward new demands, and combining is only one side of this attitude. The other sides possess equal significance, *e. g.*, the grasping by consciousness of a newly presented object (apprehension, apperception, understanding), the dividing of a whole into its parts (analysis), the taking of an intellectual attitude toward a content (judging, criticizing, deliberating, and deciding), etc.

These functions of intelligence must, then, be considered in their totality; and the actual testing of them ought not to be omitted unless we were certain that they had already been examined by implication along with some other tested function. Suppose that in a group of persons it had been possible to show that X had the best ability to combine; is it then certain that he would also take first place in other forms of activity involving intelligence and that he might, accordingly, be ranked first in total intelligence?

To ask this question is enough to insure a negative reply. I feel, I admit, that Spearman (75, 77, 80) is right in asserting that intelligence does really signify a general capacity which colors in a definite way the whole mental behavior of an individual. But we must not force this idea—nor does Spearman—so far as to assume that all the separate constituent functions of intelligence in the different fields are mechanically of equivalent degree. Such a view is, indeed, contradicted by the circumstance that there is operative in each individual bit of behavior not only a given quantity of intelligence, but also the special quality of intelligence of the person tested, and besides these a varied number of other mental traits. Thus, there are persons who have a pretty high grade of general intelligence, but who manifest it much better in analytic and critical than in synthetic work; again, there are persons in whom the receptive activities of intelligence (apprehending and understanding) are superior to the more spontaneous activities, and so on.

However, everyday life shows that we can disregard these qualitative differences and nevertheless may characterize the general grade of intelligence that a man possesses. When we do this we make, even unconsciously, certain compensations: two persons may have an intelligence of the same *value,* but of somewhat different *kinds. In tests there must be introduced a kind of systematic compensation like this.* We must test the different phases of the activity of intelligence and seek to construct a general picture of the degree of intelligence from the different results, partially accordant, partially variant as they will be.

This has given us a clear idea of what is wanted in the methodics of intelligence testing.

Negatively, it must be declared that the method of isolated tests, the idea of basing everything on a single test, is methodologically no better than such a procedure as judging the total character of a man on the strength of the single arbitrarily selected symptom of his handwriting (graphology).

Positively, three things are evident: first, *series of tests* must be arranged that will set in play the various constituent functions of intelligence; secondly, for this purpose there must be a wise *selection* of tests; out of the immense number of possible tests only those should be chosen that afford a decided and a reliable symptomatic value, general applicability, and possibility of objective evaluation; thirdly, there must be created a system by means of which the several particular results of the testing can be united into one *resultant value, i. e.,* a value that shows the grade of intelligence of the subject objectively in an inclusive formula in which performances of different degrees of value shall in some way be compensated.

3. *Series of Tests*

The first of these positive requirements has already been met for a long time since; in especial, since Rieger numerous test series have been used by the psychiatrists for testing intelligence. These series have been based as a rule upon a psychological schema, though this schema has varied a good deal from one investigator to another. For illustration two such series may be mentioned, both of them quite recent.

Sommer (26), in an article just published on the methods of intelligence testing, discusses in order the materials for testing the following aspects of the problem: relation of memory, of school information, of arithmetical ability and of association to understanding, also attention, capacity to apprehend, completeness of complexes, analysis of complexes, redintegration of complexes, mechanical knowledge (cleverness), constructive knowledge, logical subordination and superordination, notion of cause and effect, intellectual interests, understanding of the environment.

Ziehen (30), in the last (3d) edition of his *Prinzipien und Methoden der Intelligenzprüfung*, makes the following classification: retention, development and differentiation of ideas (generalization, isolation and complexion of ideas), reproduction and combination, and describes the numerous forms of questions and tests used in his clinic for each of these divisions.

Although one cannot deny that these and other series devised by psychiatrists are quite comprehensive, yet they are open to criticism in other respects: the requirements that were laid down above, under *b* and *c*, are met by them only partially or not at all. For all these series give the impression that the selection of tests may have been more a matter of chance or arbitrary choice than something determined by actual guaging of their value. As a rule the selection was based upon *a priori* reasoning that a certain capacity, *e. g.*, retention or combination, which had been assumed to belong to intelligence was 'hit' by a certain kind of test. Very seldom was any actual preliminary investigation made to see whether this particular test was really superior to so and so many others by virtue of the precision, constancy and significance of the particular values that it afforded. Moreover, this chance selection evidently explains why there is so little agreement between the test series of different investigators: every psychiatrical clinic has its own special method of testing intelligence; every specialist in nervous diseases, every physician in charge of classes for subnormals chooses his tests to suit his fancy, and thus it has been impossible, so far, to effect any real comparison, corroboration and standardization of the results of different investigators.

Finally, the usual psychiatrical test-series suffer from the lack of any principle by which to *summarize* the results in a single value. The psychiatrists recognize that it is impossible to set a value on the intelligence of a person as a whole, for they apply such predicates as "poor in judgment," "mentally feeble," "imbecile," "idiotic;" but if we watch the way in which, in the individual case, they arrive at the general conclusion that they draw from the data of their test-series, we note a yawning gap. The mosaic of test results is, and remains, only raw material; no fundamental methodological principle, but only intuition, routine and subjective estimation of their results, dictates the final decision concerning the intelligence of the subject. In a certain sense, there is an advantage in deciding in this way, for the gift—wellnigh an artistic gift—of intuitive appreciation and sympathetic understanding is peculiarly indispensable to the psychiatrist. But if we leave this possibility quite out of account, there remains a decided disadvantage, because every conclusion arrived at by this method then remains a subjective one that cannot be controlled or subjected to generalization. On this account we are justified in demanding that, at least *in addition* to this intuitive diagnosis, there should also be a method for making an objective evaluation of the results. To meet this demand these mere collocations of tests will have to be replaced by a closed system of tests which will permit the derivation of a final general index of intelligence from the results obtained from any subject whomsoever, and that in accordance with prescribed rules that can be applied in a comparable way in all places and on men of different grades of intelligence.

An alienist has come forward lately with an attempt of this sort, *i. e.*, an attempt to join together a series of tests *systematically* so as to furnish a 'picture' of an individuality. I refer to the so-called 'profile-method' of the Russian, Rossolimo (23-24a): a method that really includes more than mere tests of intelligence and comes, therefore, but partially within our scope.

Rossolimo has contrived ten tests for each of ten different mental functions. The results obtained from the single subject are set out graphically by erecting ordinates corresponding to the number of the tests achieved for each of the functions under test. The ends of these ordinates are then joined to make a curve that Rossolimo calls the 'individual profile.' This profile line is supposed to furnish a pictorial representation of the total nature of a patient. Thus, for instance, in those disorders in which the capacity of immediate reproduction is decidedly reduced while the other capacities remain unaffected, the profile will show a sharp notch at a definite point, and so on.

The tests proposed by Rossolimo have many commendable features; we may note, for example, the little puzzles, like the separating of two interlaced wire nooses, etc., that are used to test technical ability. Yet, on the whole, the principle of the construction of the profile is too superficial and the coördination of certain tests to certain mental functions, *e. g.*, to volitional acts, is not precise enough to allow us to hope for much success.

This demand for a system of tests presents such an exceedingly difficult scientific problem that it is perfectly evident that alienists and educators can not solve it as a side issue of their professional work, but that psychology itself will have to undertake the task. It is interesting in this connection to note how psychology attacked the problem along two very different lines. I feel that it is important to consider them separately in what follows. Neither of these two lines of effort should be regarded as the only correct one; each method has its advantages and its disadvantages, and, what is particularly important, each has its special aim for which it is fitted. The *method of age-gradation of Binet and Simon* permits of a rough gradation of intelligence for the whole range of development of the child; it is for use in a comparable manner with children of different ages, of different nationality and cultural level, with normal and with feeble-minded children of all grades. The *method of rank correlation,* on the other hand, is limited thus far to a comparison of the members of a small homogeneous group, but renders it possible to test the gradation of intelligence within this group with a precision that the Binet method can not approximate. A considerable amount of material is already available for the first of these methods, and we shall have to deal with it at some length for that reason. With the second method, on the contrary, our discussion will center upon the outlook for its future development.

Both methods have been tried out so far almost exclusively upon school children; but it is to be expected that they will find use also in testing the intelligence of adults, both normal and mentally deficient.

II. The Method of Age-Gradation (Binet-Simon Method[1])

1. *The Principle of the Method and the Tests Employed in It*

In the nineties Binet and Simon conceived the idea of constructing a "graded scale of intelligence" (*Echelle métrique de l'intelligence*) that should be especially planned for testing the intelligence of children. The requirements to be satisfied by the method were the following. A series of tests should be found for each year of childhood the passing of which could be considered normal and typical for children of just precisely this age. The tests must be relatively uninfluenced by external and chance conditions, especially by school learning, so that the result might bring out as purely as possible the real mental endowment of the child; they must admit of as uniform use as possible in different nations, languages or grades of culture: they should be easy to carry out, not necessitate laboratory apparatus or instruments of precision, should not exact too much

[1]Comprehensive descriptions of his method are given by Binet (partly in conjunction with Simon) in references 33 to 37. A general review of the development of the method is given by Bobertag (39). [Also recently by Meumann, *Arch. f. d. ges. Psych.*, 25: 1912 (Literatur, 85 ff.).—*Translator.*]

time of the child, should not impose hardship on him or tire him, and yet must possess sufficient accuracy to make possible comparison and checking of the investigations undertaken by different persons; and, finally, they should make it possible to work out a final value for each subject tested that could be deemed a measure of his general intelligence.

It seems, at first blush, as if the fulfilling of so many different demands would raise insurmountable difficulties. Above all, there was no preliminary information available as to what intellectual performance might be expected, even approximately, from a child of a given age. If some time you ask a teacher or some one who has been dealing with children of different ages for a long time at what age a child could be expected to give correctly the difference between two designated objects, *e. g.*, wood and glass, and at what age he would be able to explain the difference between two abstract concepts, *e. g.*, lies and mistakes, he would either be silent or make a blind guess at it. Here, then, was virgin land to explore. When to that is added the conditions that have just been stated, many of which are hard to reconcile with one another—freedom from school training, general ease of application, brevity, precision, possibility of quantitative evaluation, there can be no doubt that there was laid down here one of the hardest problems that applied psychology had set for itself up to this time.

Nevertheless, the difficulty has, in principle, been overcome. Of course this does not mean that the present form of the method can be regarded as a final form: it will doubtless suffer so many modifications in the near future that it will hardly be recognized in the end. But we know that we are on the right track, and in some future decades it can be fully appreciated what praise Binet and his co-worker Simon have deserved by directing us along this path.

A short time ago—October 18, 1911—the gifted and highly esteemed creator of the method died. His all-too-early demise, that we mourn most bitterly, compels others now to pick up the threads that he had spun. At such a moment it is appropriate to summarize briefly what has been gained and to point out the steps that are to be taken for further advance.

After many years of preliminary empirical investigation to determine what tests might be considered normal for given ages, Binet and Simon published (33) in the year 1908, the first complete account of their system or tests. It comprised a series of from five to seven tests for each age from three to thirteen years. A revised draft appeared in 1911 (35, 36) in which many tests are modified, many shifted to different age-years and the number of tests for each age-grade brought uniformly to five. The 1911 system replaces tests for 11, 12 and 13-year-olds by tests for 13 and 15-year-olds and adults.

A list of all the investigations conducted on the B. S. tests to date is given in the bibliography at the end. In the appendix there are brought together in comparative form the series of tests proposed for each age by Binet and Simon in 1908, and 1911, by Bobertag, and by Terman and Childs.

As a glance at the list of tests shows, almost all of them are of the alternative type, *i. e.*, they are tests in which performance can not be graduated, but can only be scored right or wrong (+ or —). Failure to reply at all is counted 'minus' just as much as an expressly given wrong answer. It must be admitted also that it is often quite hard to decide in a given case whether to rate an answer + or —: the only way to do this with certainty is to practise for a long time and to observe uniformly the criteria that have been chosen for the decision.

The tests are extremely varied in nature.

Memory is tested, on the one hand as immediate memory for digits and sentences of different lengths, for a story that is read, and for three simple orders given together, and on the other hand as possession of simple everyday knowledge (days of the week, months, coins, right and left). Size and availability of vocabulary is determined by the number of words that can be named in three minutes.

Since 1911 a test of suggestibility (judgment of line-lengths) has been introduced.

Motor abilities are tested by some tests of drawing from copy, paper cutting and writing. Practical accomplishments are involved in counting coins, making change for a larger coin, executing the three commissions just mentioned.

Most of the tests, however, aim more directly at intellectual activities. *Comparison* and *discrimination* are dealt with in various forms, *e. g.*, sensory comparison (of small boxes of like appearance, but unlike weight), logical discrimination from memory, both between concrete terms (wood and glass, fly and butterfly) and between abstract terms (lies and mistakes); esthetic comparison (drawings of beautiful and ugly faces). There are also tested *defining* of both concrete and abstract terms, the *completing* of omissions in a text, the *combining* of three words into a sentence, *orderly arranging* both of sensory material (putting five little boxes in order according to their weight), and of logical, verbal material (placing jumbled-up words in a sentence); the intelligent apprehension of a picture; critical apprehension, both optical (noting omissions in drawings of persons), and logical (recognizing inconsistencies in certain sentences); practical moral intelligence (by questions in the form: 'What's the thing to do when so-and-so happens?').

Many of the tests recur in different age-levels in such a way that the standard of performance demanded is varied. Thus, the pictures are presented to subjects of all ages; enumeration of the pictured objects corresponds to the 3-year old level, a description of the action that the persons are carrying on, to the 7-year old level, a comprehension of the total meaning of the picture to the 12-year old level. The defining of concrete terms appears in the 6 and the 9-year stages; in the former, definition in terms of use suffices, *e. g.*, "What is a horse?" "To ride;" in the latter something superior to this is demanded, *e. g.*, "What is a horse?" "An animal." Finally, the memory span tests for digits and sentences are graded into several classes according to their length; thus, after once hearing the digits, the 3-year old child should be able to repeat two, the 4-year three, the 7-year five, the 12-year seven digits.

The individual tests are of unequal value. Many are of exceptional merit, *e. g.*, defining, describing pictures, answering questions that put a premium on intelligence. It is also a very meritorious feature that there are tests among them whose solution does not depend on readiness in the use of speech, *e. g.*, the arrangement of the five weights, esthetic comparison, recognizing omissions in pictures: we are as a rule altogether too much inclined to identify control of verbal expression with intelligence, an inference that is often false. Others of the tests, however, are more dependent than we could wish on external, particularly on home influences, *e. g.*, knowing coins, or are too much mere functions of pure mechanical memory (reciting the days of the week), so that it would be better to supplant them by others in the future. It must be recognized that any change in the selection and arrangement of these tests presents a difficulty of quite another sort than as if they were mere collocations of tests: for, since each of these tests is a factor in the determination of the final score, it is possible that a change may destroy the equilibrium of the whole system. This is easy to be seen in the supplementary investigation of Binet and Simon themselves, when they tried to correct their system by the omission, insertion and transference of particular tests: for trials, *e. g.*, those of Terman and Childs and of Chotzen, have shown that the second edition (1911) is in many respects less useful than the earlier form (1908).

What remedies can be devised for this situation will be discussed below (Section 5a).

The *technique* of the Binet-Simon method is by no means so easy as the simplicity of the material used would lead one at first to suppose. It is to be recommended that, so far as is in any way feasible, the examiner should always do his work with the aid of an assistant to keep the record, so as to avoid the undesirable division of attention between testing and recording. Both of these experimenters must have gained a high degree of practise and be well used to one another before they proceed to actual testing. The examiner must have an almost mechanical exactness and uniformity in the formulation of the continually recurring questions, in the modulation of his voice, etc., yet he must be prepared for the many individual variations that appear in consequence of different reactions of the subjects, and must have definite measures in readiness for use in these junctures. Never must he permit it to be seen that some answers are more, others less satisfactory to him: rather must he maintain an attitude of uniform and quiet friendliness. The recorder should not confine himself to the mere noting of plus and minus signs to show the net outcome of each test, but should also note down as fully as possible what the subject says and also such features of his behavior and attitude toward the tests as are worth noting. This is necessary both because it is often impossible to decide whether to credit a test 'plus' or 'minus' until later on, after quiet consideration (and the material must be available for that) and also because it should make possible a qualitative analysis of the examinee.

The individual subject ought, of course, to be tested not only with the tests of his age, but also with a considerable part of the whole series—on account of the area of scattered distribution to be discussed in a moment. The examiner should begin with tests that are neither too easy nor too difficult, avoid monotony and introduce short pauses if fatigue becomes noticeable. The testing of a single individual takes, for normals 20 to 30 minutes, according to age and circumstances, for abnormals from one-half to three-quarters of an hour, on account of the slower response.

In mass experiments there is a source of difficulty in the possibility of communication between those already tested and those to be tested. It is true that the danger of such a 'psychic infection' is not very great, on account of the peculiar character of the material used for the testing; nevertheless, one should avoid, as far as may be, the possibility of any spreading of information. Thus, for instance, it is not advisable to test the pupils of one class on several days in succession. If it is desired to examine a rather large number of children that belong in the same group, the plan followed at Breslau seems useful: four experimenters (with their clerks), all of whom had been trained to conduct the tests in the same way, carried on tests the same afternoon in different rooms. Each experimenter could deal with four or five subjects in this time, and each subject was obliged to go home directly after his examination; in this way, 16 to 20 members of the class were tested without there being possible any exchange of ideas between them.

For all further details of the technique of these tests the directions for using them that are already available for different nations must be consulted.

Such directions have been given for the examinations of French children by Binet and Simon in 1911 (35, 36), for English and American children by Whipple in his *Manual* (28), by Wallin (67) and more briefly by Huey (9), and for Italians by Treves-Saffiotti (66). For use in Germany Lipmann first followed the original instructions as precisely as possible, and then Bobertag (40) described very fully his elaboration of them as based on practical tests—an elaboration that differs from Binet and Simon to advantage in some particulars, *e. g.*, in the choice of pictures. The extended directions for testing and questioning that Bobertag has prepared should form the basis of all future investigations in Germany.[2]

2. *The Resultant Values: Mental Age, Mental Retardation, Advance, and Arrest; Mental Quotient*

We must now pass on to note how the grade of intelligence of a subject can be derived from his performances in the tests.

Considering the problem schematically, we might think that the grade of intelligence could be ex-

[2] The simple set of materials needed for carrying on the German tests, after Bobertag (lists of questions, tests of memory span, pictures, set of small boxes for weights, etc.), may be had of the Institute for Applied Psychology at Klein-Glienicke.

pressed by the stage whose tests could just be passed by the child: a subject who readily passed all the tests up through the 9-year ones, but failed with the 10-year and subsequent ones, would, accordingly, possess a nine-year grade of intelligence.

But things are never quite so simple in actuality as they are in theory. The varying tests of any given age-level—we may call them *a. b. c. d. e,*—are not all equally difficult for all children, but there are, on the contrary, quite remarkable individual variations. One child passes *a* to *d,* but fails with *e;* another passes *a, c* and *e,* but not *b* and *d.* This is due in part to momentary fluctuations of attention, fatigue, etc., that must, of course, always be reckoned with, but in part also to qualitative differences in intelligence. The correlation between the different phases of intellectual functions is truly never so high that a positive accomplishing of test *a* must necessarily entail a like accomplishing of the approximately 'equally diffcult' tests *b, c* and *d.*

And so it comes about that there is no hard and fast boundary between the age-level that a child passes completely and the levels that are unquestionably beyond his powers; rather is there an intermediate territory of greater or less extent within which successes and failures are scattered in irregular fashion: we shall call this the area of irregularity (*Gebiet der Staffelstreuung*). It is impossible to derive a mean or average value from the data afforded by this area without proceeding in a somewhat arbitrary manner, but the formula proposed by Binet and Simon seems to have answered very well so far.

According to it, one first ascertains up to what age-level the tests are passed without failure (save that possible failure with a single test is not counted, because such failure may have been due to a momentary lapse of attention). This age-level is taken as the basis, but every five tests passed in levels above it are counted as one more year. If, then, a child should pass all tests (save a single one) to and including the six-year level and in addition three tests each in the 7th, the 8th, and the 9th year and one test also in the 10th year, these ten additional tests would be counted as two years, and the child would obtain for the net value of his intelligence, 6 + 2 years, *i. e.*, his intelligence would be rated as that of an 8-year old child.

This net value in terms of which the total intelligence of the subject is graded has, therefore, the significance of an age-designation: it indicates that the intelligence of the child tested is equivalent to the average intelligence of the children of the age stated. We thus arrive at the concept of *mental age* (*Intelligenzalter, niveau intellectuel*), which is the cardinal feature of the method of graded tests.

Now mental age must not, of course, be thought of as an absolutely unequivocal determination of a subject's intelligence, but only as a very rough quantitative characterization of its value, without any implication as to qualitative differences, because one and the same mental age can be figured from the most varied sorts of distribution of passed and failed tests. But this very thing appears to constitute an advantage, rather than a disadvantage of the concept of mental age, for it gives expression to a fundamental psychological fact (already mentioned above) that, on account of the purely formal character of intelligence and the lack of complete correlation among its constituent capacities, there never is a real phenomenological equivalence between the intelligence of two persons: what we do have is rather a teleological equivalence—when measured in terms of the single function of all intelligence, namely, adaptation to new requirements. And for this equivalence of two intelligences mental age furnishes an approximate measure, despite the fact that their equivalence does not mean their identity.

The area of irregularity yet further affects the computation of mental age and in a way to which sufficient attention has not always been given. In order to equalize possible omissions in the lower test-levels, one must always have at one's disposal tests in higher levels. Now the original Binet-Simon series comprised tests up to 13 years only: it follows that mental age 12 or 13 cannot be correctly computed, for tests from yet higher levels might perhaps have raised the total performance to a higher value. In using the 1908 Binet series, accordingly, computations ought to be carried up to mental age eleven only.

The area of irregularity, again, affords another value in addition to mental age, viz.: the *range of irregularity* (*Streuungsbreite*). A child whose successes and failures are strewn irregularly over test-levels from 6 to 10 years has the same mental age, to be sure, but a very different range of irregularity, when compared with another whose mixture of successes and failures lies in the 7th to the 9th years only. Bobertag, who first gave attention to the importance of differences in ranges of irregularity, has devised a way of computing this factor; I have myself suggested another way, but neither has been published as yet.

Yet, even with these methods, qualitative differences in the area of irregularity are not touched, and for this reason it will be necessary in many cases to enter into a detailed *analysis* of the testing as well as to state the two resultant values (mental age and range of irregularity). It will often be distinctly worth while to determine in which tests there was special difficulty, in which special success. Moreover, the value of observing the child during the testing must not be underestimated, for in many of the tests there are ways of setting about the task that may be of great interest (and for medical or pedagogical judgment of the case, too), though these things would not be evident in the mere plus or minus set down for the outcome of the tests. We may allude, in this connection, among other things, to the kind of description given to the pictures, to the enumeration of the 60 words, as well as to the behavior of the child when he arranges in order the five weights of like appearance but unlike weight. In this last it is not nearly so important whether the child finally gets the order right as it is to observe the child's manner of going to work—whether and how quickly he grasps the unaccustomed problem, whether he compares just two weights each time, or compares each weight with all the others when he puts it in place, or what not. In these investigations we should be warned, then, against the bare pursuit of numerical values: computation of such values and qualitative analysis must supplement one another, though, naturally, now the former and now the latter will receive special stress, according to the setting of the problem.

But let us return to mental age. The full significance of this final value is disclosed only when we consider it in relation to other circumstances. It can evidently be related to other quantitative scales, like chronological age, school grade and school standing, or we can find out how it varies with certain qualitative conditions, like social level, type of school, nationality and the like.

Doubtless most significant is the relation of mental age to the actual *chronological age* of the subject, for, as already said, a certain mental level goes normally with a certain age, so that the relation of mental to chronological age indicates the amount of discrepancy between the intelligence present and that required (in the sense of a norm to be expected), and in this way affords an expression for the degree of the child's intellectual endowment.

Up to now this discrepancy has always been computed in the simple form of the difference between the two ages, which, when negative gave the absolute *mental retardation,* when positive the absolute *mental advance* of the child in terms of years. Thus, if mental retardation = — 2, the child's mental development is two years behind the normal level of his age.

It is perfectly clear how valuable the measurement of mental retardation is, particularly in the investigation of abnormal children. It has, however, been shown recently that the simple computation of the absolute difference between the two ages is not entirely adequate for this purpose, because this difference does not mean the same thing at different ages (compare what is said in Section 4a, pp. 70 ff.) . Only when children of approximately equal age-levels are under investigation can this value suffice: for all other cases the introduction of the *mental quotient* will be recommended farther on (cf. pp. 80 ff.). This value expresses not the difference, but the ratio of mental to chronological age and is thus partially independent of the absolute magnitude of chronological age. The formula is, then: mental quotient = mental age ÷ chronological age. With children who are just at their normal level, the value is 1, with those who are advanced, the value is greater than unity, with those mentally retarded, a proper fraction. The more pronounced the feeble-mindedness, the smaller the value of the fraction.

Another and last concept that 'mental age' supplies is that of *mental arrest.* This applies only to feeble-minded individuals and means a mental age that is not exceeded, despite increase of chronological age.

3. *Results with Normal Children*

The investigation of normal children forms a precondition of the whole method, since the norm for each age must first be determined upon them. Yet, at the same time, investigations of these children have already brought out a series of results that permit us to set no slight value on the future worth of intelligence tests for the problems of normal pedagogy. Thus far, tests have been made chiefly upon children in the common schools of both sexes and of different ages, less often upon pupils of the higher schools.

(*a*) *General distribution of the level of intelligence.* In those investigations where there have been tested a large number of elementary school pupils of different ages and with no attempt at special selection, there could be worked out general statistics of the number of children that are at, above or below the mental level of their age. I bring together in the following table the percentages thus far obtained.

TABLE I.

DISTRIBUTION OF THE LEVEL OF INTELLIGENCE FOR ALL AGES COLLECTIVELY.

Difference, in Years, Between Mental and Chronological Age	−2	−1	0	+1	+2
Binet (203 Children)	6.	21.5	51	20.5	1.
Bobertag (261 Children)[3]	3.	19	52	22.5	2.5
Goddard (1277 Children)[4]	11[5]	20.5	41.5	21.5	5.5[5]

[3]Children from 5 to 10 years old.
[4]Children from 5 to 11 years old.
[5]Includes two or more years below or above age.

Binet (37, p. 112) has brought together a frequency distribution of 203 normal children (ages not given). In this distribution we may note a remarkable symmetry: almost exactly one-half of the children are 'at age,' a good quarter are 'below age,' and a scant quarter are 'above age.'

Bobertag has called attention to this peculiarly simple symmetrical numerical distribution that he had noted first in his own results and then found confirmed in Binet.

Bobertag has just published his own frequency distribution. I take from it (40, II, Table I) the figures for 261 children between 5 and 10 years. While here, again, the 'at age' children comprise half of all the cases, the divergence between the two other groups is but slight—the 'advanced' are somewhat more numerous than the 'retarded' children.

A third set of data, derived from a much more extensive material, has been given us by Goddard (48), who has tested all the school children of a small American city (Vineland, N. J.). The distribution curve that Goddard has prepared from his raw figures is certainly not usable, because he has included in it also the age-levels of 12 years and over, *i. e.*, children for whom no more adequate tests were available from higher levels; the data for these subjects must therefore necessarily be thrown out. If we bring together only those children whose area of irregularity is of satisfactory scope, children, then, between 4 and 11 years old, we shall have 1277 children, and it is their percentual distribution that I have computed. In it the percentage of children 'at age' is somewhat less, that of children 'above age' is approximately the same as Bobertag, while that of children 'below age' shows a plain, though not very large increase.

When we stop to think that we have to do in these three investigations not only with children of different nationality, but also with different examiners, each of whom had his own way of setting the tests and of evaluating them, we can not lay great stress upon what discrepancy exists between the three sets of statistics: we may conclude from them that *when a sufficiently large number of non-selected children of different ages are tested, their degree of intelligence will be distributed in a somewhat symmetrical fashion.* Approximately one-half (in America a scant half) stand at the level of their age; about a fifth (to a fourth) are a year retarded and the like number a year advanced; only a small percentage (at the most 11 per cent.) show more than one year of retardation and a still smaller fraction (at the most 5.5 per cent.) is mentally advanced by more than one year.

One must be careful not to regard the 'at age' child and the 'normal' child as synonymous terms: on the contrary, the statistical results themselves show that the 'at age' children simply constitute the middle section of normality, while the children that are one year advanced or retarded are still completely within the bounds of normality.

It is worth noting that the distribution just cited bears a certain resemblance to the simplest type of distribution known as Gauss' frequency curve, for this latter is not only a symmetrical curve, but it is also divided by the value known as the 'probable error' into three sections, and in such a manner that the middle section comprises the half, and the two end-sections each one-quarter of all the cases. Even a generation ago Galton advanced the hypothesis that the abilities of a large group of non-selected individuals would be distributed symmetrically in the form of the Gaussian curve. It is true that Galton thought the Gaussian law of distribution could be extended to apply to a very detailed gradation (16 grades) of ability, whereas statistics at present available only make it probable for a few main groups.

Bobertag has supplemented our knowledge of this matter by discovering that a similar distribution holds good on other occasions when a fairly large number of individuals is divided into good, medium and poor groups. In statistics of marks pertaining to 2772 pupils, it turned out that marks of "better than satisfactory" were assigned to 25.7 per cent., of "satisfactory" to 50.8 per cent., and of "unsatisfactory" to 23.5 per cent. of all cases (40, II, Table IV).

Yet it is well not to ascribe too great significance to these ratios of distribution. In the first place, the empirical data now at our disposal are not enough to warrant as yet the assumption of a general conformity to law; and even for the data now at our disposal the formula holds only as a rough approximation and merely as a general tendency for a rather large number of cases within which the numerous irregularities compensate each other (compare on this point the next section). Nevertheless, the findings already secured are of sufficient interest to be followed up farther.[6]

---

[6]Further discussion of this principle of symmetrical distribution and its relation to the Gaussian curve may be found in one of my previous articles (I, 248 ff.) and in Bobertag (40, II).

The principle governing this distribution has, however, heuristic value even now in two ways: (1) When we are obliged to divide a group of persons on the basis of their mental ability into a good, a medium, and a poor group, the convenient and common division into three groups of equal size is certainly less close to the actual gradations than the setting off of a good and a poor quarter from the homogeneous middle half of medium ability. (2) A requirement, *e. g.*, of a test or of a series of tests, may stand as normal for a given group of individuals when approximately 75 per cent. of the members of the group meet it in a satisfactory or more than satisfactory manner. This idea has been used by Bobertag[7] for the standardization of tests.

(*b*) *Different age-levels and nationalities.* Goddard has thought that the symmetry of the curve of which we have just been speaking might be deemed proof that the Binet-Simon arrangement of tests represents in a way an ideal series, because it has afforded on empirical test a distribution that was theoretically to have been expected. But this conclusion is unjustifiable. The curve of symmetry applies primarily only to all children taken collectively, without regard to age; but the Binet-Simon tests should really embrace normal standards for children of every one of the series of ages and their correctness would be demonstrated only provided the symmetrical distribution were disclosed for normal unselected children of each single year. But this is by no means the case, and, as a matter of fact,

---

[7]See Section 5a for details.

least of all in Goddard's own results. Rather is it true, as is evident from closer consideration, that the symmetrical curve above mentioned owes its existence to the fact that the varying results of different years practically compensate each other.[8] In truth, the results of almost all who have tried out the Binet-Simon method, regardless of the nationality tested, agree that *the series set for the lower years are too easy, those for the higher too difficult.* The evidence for this, so far as known to me, I have introduced in Table II.

From Goddard's (48, p. 243), Bobertag's (40, II, Table I) and Miss Johnstone's[9] raw tables I have computed the percentages of frequency for American, German and English children. Goddard's data I have figured for each year separately; those for the two other investigators by bringing two or three years together, on account of the smaller number of cases (Table II). It will be seen that in the lower years many more are 'advanced' than there should be: in Goddard and in Johnstone the advanced outnumber not only the retarded, but even the 'at-age' children. Thus, for instance, in Goddard more than half the 5-year old children attain a mental age of 6 years or over—clear evidence that these tests are much too easy. In Bobertag the lack of symmetry is not so pronounced.

The area of excessive percentage of advanced children (and thus of excessive ease of the tests) extends in Goddard through the 7th, in Bobertag through the 8th year; in Johnstone it has not entirely disappeared even at the 9th year. Then comes a sudden reversal: in the higher years the number of retarded children increases: the tests are therefore too hard.

With the 155 subjects examined by Bloch and Preiss (38) there was made at the outset a selection such that only children of medium ability and school performance were tested. Consequently, retardation in mental age appeared almost not at all, but advance did appear, though in diminishing frequency with advancing age.

[8]Ayres (31) calls attention to this point in his critique of Goddard.

[9]In Miss Johnstone's original work (52) the quantitative data are not given sufficiently clearly, but these data are given by Binet (36, p. 196) where will be found a table of distribution for 146 Sheffield school girls as imparted in a letter from Miss Johnstone.

From the data given it can be computed that there were above the level of their age a full 50 per cent. of the 7-year olds, 20 per cent. of the 8 and 9-year olds and only 14 per cent. of the 10 and 11-year olds.

TABLE II.

PERCENTAGES RETARDED, AT AGE AND ADVANCED AT DIFFERENT YEARS.

Investigator	Chronological Age	Retarded	At Age	Advanced
Goddard	5	12	35	53
	6	20.5	30	49.5
	7	13	58	29
	8	44	41	15
	9	40	28	32
	10	27.5	56	16.5
	11	56	36	8
Bobertag	5-6	11	60	29
	7-8	7	48.5	44.5
	9-11	34	50	16
Johnstone	6-7	12	20	68
	8-9	20	40	40
	10-11	62	25	13

In the work of the Americans, Terman and Childs (64), and of Mlle. Descoeudres (46), of Geneva, we find another method of presenting data, but the same result. The first-named tested 396 unselected children and figured the average value of each age; they found that the young children attained a much too high level, the older children a too low average level of intelligence, so that, on the whole, the mental levels were more like one another than were the chronological levels. It follows that the tests fail to bring fully to light the actual differences between the children. Mlle. Descoeudres had tested in all only 24 children of six different ages; the results showed differences of only two to four years in the mental ages of children in the youngest and oldest groups, though the chronological ages differed by six years.

All these findings show, first of all, that the arrangement of the tests set forth by Binet and Simon in 1908 suffer from not inconsiderable errors that must be removed. Binet himself has recognized these defects, too, at least in part, for he subsequently relegated the tests for 11, 12 and 13-year subjects to higher age-levels.

TABLE III.

AVERAGES FOR CERTAIN YEARS. (TERMAN AND CHILDS.)

Chronological Age	Mental Age
4.75	6.50
7.50	8.00
12.33	11.00

But far more important is a positive result, viz.: the *international accordance* in the judgment as to special ease or special difficulty of certain test-levels. It is certainly not of minor significance that the 6-year old tests were too easy and the 11-year old as uniformly too difficult, with the 8 and 9-year old apparently forming a between-lying zone in the case of children in the common schools of America, Germany, France and England, all without exception. That, despite the differences in race and language, despite the divergences in school organization and in methods of instruction, there should be so decided agreement in the reactions of the children—is, in my opinion, the best vindication of the *principle* of the tests that one could imagine, because this agreement demonstrates that *the tests do actually reach and discover the general developmental conditions of intelligence* (so far as these are operative in public school children of the present cultural epoch), and not mere fragments of knowledge and attainments acquired by chance.

And this confirmation of the principle may also lead us confidently to expect that the discrepancies that have been revealed at the same time in some of the details of the system can be obviated in the future.

(c) *Children of different social strata.* Social differences turn out otherwise than do differences of nationality, for they come out more or less conspicuously in the results of the tests. The task of making comparative investigations by the graded tests of children of different social levels was undertaken in 1910 by Binet (36, p. 187) and by Breslau teachers, simultaneously.

The incentive that led Binet to undertake this problem arose in certain investigations conducted by Decroly and Mlle. Degand in a private school at Brussels (45), the results of which seemed to cast a measure of doubt upon the value of Binet's tests, since the tests turned out, all of them, to be too easy. To be explicit, of 45 children tested, no one was below, 9 were at, and the rest were above the level of their age (13 by one year, 17 by two years, and 9 even by three years).[10] Binet now points out, and rightly, that these figures present no argument whatsoever against the value of his tests, but merely afford a positive contribution to the study of the differentiation conditioned by social factors. For all these Belgian children were sprung from the circles of the cultured middle class, whereas the Parisian children to whom the tests were 'fitted' belonged to lower classes. Binet, on this basis, reckons the average difference in mental age between children of the higher and lower classes at approximately a year and a half. Of course, this figure can stand only as a rough approximation; it will vary, particularly at different levels of chronological age—a

[10]See the review by Bobertag, *Zeits. f. angew. Psych.*, 5: p. 205.

point to which Binet, unfortunately, does not refer.

Binet, himself, also induced some school directors of his acquaintance to take up this question in Paris. As a matter of fact, children in the superior schools were not considered, and the attempt was made merely to ascertain whether an influence of social environment could be discerned *within the common schools.* It is to be regretted that these tests were carried out upon but an extraordinarily small number of children.

One investigation (p. 194) that was restricted to a single school came to no result. In this study there were examined 54 children, classified into four groups on the basis of social status. It may be mere accident that relatively more advanced children were found among the poorest than among the other groups; but at any rate there was no trace of any positive relationship between mental age and social position. Probably, as Binet himself has already pointed out, the social differences present in this study were too small to affect the outcome.

TABLE IV.

DISTRIBUTION OF TWO GROUPS OF 30 PUBLIC SCHOOL CHILDREN EACH.

	Retarded			Advanced	
	2 Years	1 Year	At Age	1 Year	2 Years
Poor Neighborhood....	1	11	13	4	1
Good Neighborhood....	1	3	10	10	6

On the other hand, a clear difference was revealed when comparison was made of two public schools (p. 198), one of which was situated in the poorest quarter, the other in a relatively well-to-do neighborhood of Paris. There were tested from each school 30 children of corresponding ages, selected without reference to their school performance. Table IV shows how much more numerous were the cases of retarded intelligence in the poorer school. Binet figures the average superiority in mental age of the children of the better situated school to be three quarters of a year.[11]

A question as interesting as it is difficult to answer arises when we seek the causes of these differences in performance. It would obviously be very premature to assume as already positively demonstrated that the intelligence, considered as innate mental ability, was of lower grade in children of the lower and poorer classes. Of course, it is not impossible that this may have been operative as a causal factor. One might, perhaps, assume that the very rise into the higher and better-off classes would itself predicate a certain intellectual selection, and that thus the children of these classes would have come into the world equipped with a superior intellectual endowment.

But, on the other hand, it must be remembered that no series of tests, however skillfully selected it may be, does reach the innate intellectual endowment, stripped of all complications, but rather this endowment in conjunction with all the influences to

[11]Since Stern assembled this material there has appeared an American study that does not confirm the general principle of environmental influence (J. Weintrob and R. Weintrob. The Influence of Environment on Mental Ability as Shown by Binet-Simon Tests. *Jour. of Educ. Psych.*, 3: 1912, 577-583). The subjects were 210 children, 70 from the Horace Mann School of Teachers College, Columbia University, representing children from wealthy, or at least very well-to-do families, 70 from the Speyer School, representing families of the "comfortable middle class" (wage-earners and small-business men), and 70 from the Hebrew Sheltering Orphan Asylum of New York, who were children springing from a very unfavorable environment. While the relatively small number of cases and the difference of nationality may render the outcome less conclusive, the results from the three institutions "showed very small and inconsistent differences." The original article should be consulted for further analysis of the data.—*Translator.*

which the examinee has been subjected up to the moment of the testing. And it is just these external influences that are different in the lower social classes. Children of higher social status are much more often in the company of adults, are stimulated in manifold ways, are busy in play and amusements with things that require thinking, acquire a totally different vocabulary and a notable command of language, and receive better school instruction; all this must bring it about that they meet the demands of the tests better than children of the uncultured classes.

Presumably, each of these factors, internal and external, endowment and environmental influences, plays a rôle in the result; but we shall have to wait until very many, more extensive investigations have been made before we can secure more exact knowledge of the actual amount and range of influence possessed by the one or the other of them. The way to approach this problem is by special analysis of the data: it will be necessary to find out in which tests the superiority of the children of the cultured classes is particularly evident and which tests are passed with equal facility by children of both classes.

The material for a preliminary comparison of this sort has been drawn by Binet (36, p. 191) from the tables of Decroly and Degand. In them it is very interesting to note that the special superiority shown by better situated children is in those tests that involve thinking in the true sense of the term—apprehension, comparison, criticism, formation of concepts, synthesis, etc., though, it must be admitted, most of them put a premium on linguistic readiness. The tests here included are: description and explanation of pictures, comparison of two objects, definition of abstract terms, recognition of omissions in drawings, criticism of absurd statements, arrangements of the five weights, naming 60 words in three minutes. To these are to be added certain tests that obviously depend more upon external circumstances, like knowing the days of the week, the months of the year and coins. On the other hand, the tests that Binet designates as revealing social differences only slightly are for the most part those that hinge on school instruction, as copying, writing from dictation, counting backwards, making change, drawing a diamond. Only a single one of the tests that fail to reveal social differences is a real test of intelligence—the completion of gaps in a text. However, in view of the small number of children that could be used to base these results upon, any generalization of the conclusions from them is to be avoided.

This problem of social differences and their effect upon intelligence leads over directly to certain practical pedagogical principles. We may think, in this connection, for instance, of the demand [in Germany] for the establishment of the 'common' school (*Einheitsschule*), in which children of all classes of society shall be included without distinction.[12] It seems to me that in the discussion of this problem, just as in the problem of co-education, the purely psychological presuppositions are kept too little in mind because the socio-ethical phase of the question tends to claim first attention.

But how the psychological methods of testing intelligence can become of direct service for these practical questions will be shown, I hope, by an investigation with the Binet-Simon tests that is now being undertaken by a group of teachers in Breslau. The problem under study is that of a systematic comparison of pupils in a *Volksschule* and those in a *Vorschule, i. e.,* the younger pupils in the *Vorschule* of a *Gymnasium*.[13] The aim is to find out whether

[12]See the footnote on p. 53.—*Translator.*

[13]As it is impossible to render these terms in English equivalents, it is proper to explain that the German *Volksschule* is the elementary public school attended by children of the laboring or lower business classes. In it attendance is absolutely compulsory

there exist typical differences of intelligence between groups of children of the same age, and what magnitude these differences attain at different ages. In Prussia pupils may enter the *Sexta* (lowest class) of the *Gymnasium* after three years in the *Vorschule*, but only after four years in the *Volksschule*. The tests were also aimed to discover to what extent this rule is psychologically justified, not only by the differences in the curricula of the two schools, but also by the general mental maturity of the children.

Five groups were tested that had been carefully planned to be comparable in the matter of age, viz.: 7 and 9 year old pupils of the *Vorschule*, and 7, 9 and 10 year old pupils in the *Volksschule*—in all about 150 boys. (See above, pp. 35 f., for some of the precautionary rules observed in testing). The results are now being worked out; but, thanks to the courtesy of the investigators, I have been able to get some of

---

from 6 to 14, unless the child is otherwise instructed. The *Gymnasium* is one of a number of so-called 'higher' or 'secondary' schools with a 9-year curriculum (ages 9 to 18, or more), and preparatory for entrance into the university. Children of the better classes, destined for higher education, enter the *Gymnasium* (or some variant of it) after a preliminary three-year training (ages 6 to 9) in a *Vorschule*, which is thus virtually a special elementary school for better-class children. Relatively infrequently do children started in the *Volksschule* later enter the *Gymnasium*.

A demand is now being made by certain interests in Germany for the abolishment of these distinctions, at least in part, by compelling all children to begin school instruction in the same school (*Einheitsschule*)—a proposal which has been, and is, the occasion of very active, and even bitter discussion.

I have given a somewhat fuller explanation of the German school system in Appendix II of my translation of Offner's *Mental Fatigue*, an earlier number of this series of Educational Psychology Monographs.—*Translator*.

them now, and from them I have prepared the figures that appear in Table V. These figures, which must be regarded as strictly provisional, merely indicate with what percentual frequency all the tests, taken collectively, for which I have the data, have been passed, and this, it should be noted, for the three older groups of children only.[14]

TABLE V.

PERCENTAGE OF TESTS PASSED IN CERTAIN AGE-LEVELS AT BRESLAU.

	9-12	9 and 10	11 and 12
9-Year Vorschule Pupils............	70	77	64
9-Year Volksschule Pupils..........	60	81	34
10-Year Volksschule Pupils..........	70	86	46

The first column shows that the 9-year old *Volksschule* pupils rank in the number of tests passed 10 per cent. below the pupils of the same age in the better school, while the 10-year old *Volksschule* pupils attain the same measure of success as the *Vorschule* pupils a year younger. That, however, there is no real equality in this relationship is shown by the two other columns in which the percentage for the easier tests (9 and 10 levels) and the harder ones (levels 11 and 12) are calculated separately. While, in the easier tasks the *Vorschule* pupils, curiously enough, rank a little below the *Volksschule* pupils of their own age and 9 per cent. below the older pupils in that school, the outcome is quite different when we pass to the harder tasks (third column). These tests which lie above the age-level of the subjects are passed by the *Vorschule* pupils nearly twice as well as by their mates of like age in the *Volksschule*,

[14]For many very important tests, as for instance, description of the pictures, no results are at my disposal yet.

and even the older pupils in these tests fall 18 per cent. behind the younger children of the better school. If this interesting result should be confirmed again in the detailed computations, as it probably will be, we should then say: children of different social classes differ from each other less in the performances appropriate to their age than in the mastery of tasks that really lie above their level. We would have, then, a numerical demonstration for that well-known early ripening of children of the higher classes, for the anticipation of phenomena of developmental stages yet to come before the content of the current stage of development is fully exhausted.

We may look forward with interest to the final result of these investigations.

The material of Table V also furnishes further confirmation of a law of differential psychology: the more complex a mental function, the more difficult to bring it into action, the later its appearance in the course of development, then so much the greater is its variability, and so much the more definitely are men and groups of men differentiated by it (cf. 1, pp. 258 and 269).

(*d*) *Intelligence and school performance.* The relation of these two factors is easily the most important problem presented by our theme for practical pedagogy. For at this point we may hope to get an insight into the factors that condition the progress of children within the school, the place that they take among their fellow-pupils on the basis of their work, and the way their marks turn out. People are generally inclined to think there is a very close connection between intellectual ability and school ability: good pupils are forthwith regarded as intelligent, and good school work is, with a certain obviousness, expected of intelligent children, poor school work of the poor groups. So long, of course, as we had no special means of testing intelligence, there was no foundation on which to build up more exact knowledge of these interrelations: we had to content ourselves with opinions and with the generalization of occasional observations.

But now we are beginning to get on firmer ground. Tests of intelligence have already taught us that *the relations between intelligence and school ability are by no means so strict and uniform* as most persons had thought. Just here we are concerned with the conclusions reached by the Binet-Simon method with normal children, but we shall encounter the same result later on in two places (II, 4c and III, 3).

We have two measures for the school capacity of a child that we want to compare with his intelligence—his pedagogical age and his marks.

Pedagogical age is the normal age of the class to which the child belongs. If we assume that schooling begins at 6, then the pedagogical age of a class that is just entering upon its fourth school year is $6 + 3 = 9$ years. If there is in this class a child 11 years old, he then has a pedagogical retardation of two years, while an 8-year old classmate has an advancement, or acceleration, of one year. The latter is very rare with us, on account of the exact way in which promotions are regulated; cases of it appear mostly when a child enters after private preparation or from another school. Outside of Germany cases of pedagogical advance seem to be more common. Retardations are, however, quite frequent in consequence of non-promotion, long illness, etc., and sometimes they reach a considerable degree.

Comparisons of pedagogical and mental age have been made by Binet and by Goddard.

TABLE VI.

RELATION OF PEDAGOGICAL AND MENTAL AGE (BINET).

	Mental Age			
Pedagogical Age	Retarded	At Level	Advanced	Total
Retarded	14	9	1	24
Normal	16	33	16	65
Advanced	0	5	7	12
Total	30	47	24	101

Binet (36, p. 162) presents a distribution-table for 101 pupils and regards the agreement as tolerably satisfactory (Table VI). In fact, we do note that there are no paradoxical cases: no one of the children with mental retardation is pedagogically advanced, and only a single mentally advanced child turns out to be pedagogically retarded (and that case may be conditioned by illness). Yet in the remainder of the Table there are divergences of considerable magnitude: only a scant third of the mentally advanced are also pedagogically advanced; less than half of the mentally retarded are likewise pedagogically retarded, while, of the pupils 'at age' pedagogically, one quarter surpass and another quarter fall short of the mental level of their age.

An exact computation of these relations can be made by using the method of contingency.[15] Con-

[15]The formula for it is developed in another of my treatises (1, 308 ff.).

tingency means the degree of correspondence between two intersecting groups. If all children pedagogically retarded should also exhibit mental retardation, or if the converse should occur, then the contingency would be absolute (= 1); if among the pedagogically retarded children there were relatively no more mentally retarded than among the children with normal or with superior school attainments, then the contingency would be = 0. The degree of correspondence can be shown by a number lying between 0 and 1, termed the coefficient of contingency.

From the above tables I have computed the following values:

First Factor	*Second Factor*	*Degree of Correspondence*
Pedagogical retardation	Mental retardation	0.41
Mental retardation	Pedagogical retardation	0.30
Pedagogical advance	Mental advance	0.45
Mental advance	Pedagogical advance	0.19

The index of correspondence, then, is but moderately large at best and even that only when we pass from school ability to intelligence, not in the reverse direction. Hence, to draw conclusions about school status from varying intellectual abilities is even less permissible than to draw conclusions about intellectual ability from varying school status.

In his mass-experiment, Goddard (48) came to a similar result. He found that more than the half of all the children tested were in classes that did not correspond to their mental age—most of them, as a matter of fact, in a lower and only a few in a higher class.

Bobertag compared mental age with the school

marks (40, II, p. 501, Table II). In his table of distribution (Table VII), too, there are no paradoxical cases. As for the rest, the coefficients of contingency are, according to my calculation, higher than with Binet, but still, however, of only moderate magnitude:

TABLE VII

RELATION OF MENTAL AGE AND SCHOOL MARKS (BOBERTAG)

School Marks	Mental Age: Retarded	At Level	Advanced	Total
Poor	29	17	0	46
Satisfactory	26	79	21	126
Good	0	13	31	44
Total	55	109	52	216

First Factor	*Second Factor*	*Correspondence*
Poor marks	Mental retardation	0.52
Mental retardation	Poor marks	0.40
Good marks	Mental advance	0.59
Mental advance	Good marks	0.47

Here, again, it appears that inference from school performance to mental ability is safer than from mental ability to school performance, though here the correspondence between intelligence and the school performance is not so slight as with Binet, as above cited.

What, now, is the significance of this lack of complete agreement between school efficiency and the outcome of the tests of intelligence?

In the first place one might say that this was another proof of the defectiveness of the tests. That, since pedagogical age and school marks are the condensed formulation or expression of the long-continued and many-sided efficiency of the child and hence much more characteristic than the outcome of a half-hour's testing, we would place confidence in the latter only if it agreed with the former; that if it did not, then the tests or at least the gradation derived from them would amount to nothing.

Now we have already alluded in what has gone before to the weakness of the gradations of intelligence discovered by the Binet-Simon method, and it is entirely probable that this insufficiency has contributed in part to the lack of agreement with school performances.[16] Since, for example, the tests for 7-year old children are too easy, many less gifted 7-year old children will reach the level of their age as a result of the testing, although they do not rank as "satisfactory" in the school. With the older children the reverse will obtain. Nevertheless, I do not think that this is the only cause of the lack of agreement: the true cause lies in something more fundamental.

In the second place, one might believe that a true picture of mental endowment was given only by the tests, and that the blame for the disagreement should be ascribed entirely to the school; that the teachers had estimated the pupils wrongly when they assigned them marks not in accord with their mental level, and had treated them wrongly when they kept them back in a class beyond which they should have gone according to their mental level. In this vein, for instance, Goddard writes, for he refers this phenomenon almost entirely to a faulty system of promotion (48, pp. 241 and 249).

But to dispose of the matter in that way is to "pour out the baby with the bath." Of course, the

[16] This point has been made by Bobertag and others as well.

teachers, being human, make mistakes and not a few of the measures they adopt may be based upon mistaken judgment of the mental maturity of the pupil, but it is inconceivable that half of all children should be victims of such mistakes.

It seems to me, rather, that the results we have just been discussing themselves show that both of the opinions just cited are wrong. Complete agreement between school ability and intellectual ability is not to be expected at all nor even to be desired *because performance in the school depends not only upon intelligence, but also upon certain other and quite different factors.* Thus, strength of memory, which, as is well known, is correlated only to a moderate degree with intelligence, certainly plays a large—perhaps a too large—rôle in the carrying on of school activities and in the estimate of their worth; the various special talents, too, cut across and modify the action of general intelligence. But beside this there are concerned factors that have nothing at all to do with intellect, but belong to the domain of will, in the widest sense of that term: I mean the degree and duration of attention, industry and conscientiousness, sense of duty and capacity to fit into the social group.

These are the essential elements that must be added to intelligence in order to transform mere potential to actual accomplishment, and these same elements are enough, even when conjoined with intellectual ability of lesser degrees, to produce efficiency of a worthy degree. This is true in life, and it is true also even in the school; and it is good that for once these relations should be brought out clearly by numerical evidence. For the figures in the tables above do show just this, that intelligence is never more than a partial factor in school activity: and this demonstration may serve to refute that one-sided intellectualism that notes and values in pupils only their intellectual ability. Not that intellectual endowment is not still to be regarded as a factor of chief importance: in truth when by tests of intelligence and other psychological devices we shall have obtained a more exact knowledge of it, there will be much of profit for the schools and many mistakes and wrong courses of procedure can be prevented, and this so much the more as we get clear ideas of the range and limits of its meaning and importance. If, for instance, a given pupil shows only a moderate success in the tests of intelligence but does distinctly good work at school, and if there is no chance that a special talent might have exerted a decided influence (which could easily be recognized if existent), then there is a probability approximating to certainty that this pupil's strength is to be sought primarily in qualities of character and will.

Accordingly, the lack of agreement between tests of intelligence and school performance is really calculated to increase our confidence in the psychological test-methods. In this connection Kramer very pertinently remarks.[17] "Had we found a strict parallelism between the results of the testing of intelligence and the school performance, we should

[17]See reference 54, pp. 30-31. Kramer was alluding to the examination of abnormal children, but what he says applies to normal cases as well.

have had to have felt the greatest distrust of the method. It would have raised the suspicion that we were doing nothing more than testing the school attainments themselves, either directly or indirectly, in which event the method would be futile for testing native endowment and its application would be superfluous, for we would need only to resort to the school performance directly for the information."

(*e*) *Sex differences.* Comparisons of the mental abilities of boys and girls have already been carried out in large numbers in experimental psychology, but they have been almost entirely confined to single tests,[18] whereas the Binet-Simon serial tests have been used to but a surprisingly slight extent in the comparison of the sexes and have not yet led to positive conclusions. I confine myself to a brief exposition of the material in question.

Goddard tested 835 boys and 712 girls. Unfortunately, he has thrown together the data for the different ages: it follows that his figures (48, p. 250) lose much of their value for comparative purposes, because retardation and advance have quite different meanings at different age-levels. Nevertheless, we may reproduce here the table of distribution for the children (which I have converted into percents).

The tabular results suggest a slight inferiority of the boys, most evident in the group of those retarded

[18]The literature has been brought together by me elsewhere (1: Bibliography, Section VI); here we may cite the general summaries of the results of tests by Meyer and Wreschner, and the extensive original studies of Cohn and Dieffenbacher (Nos. 1048, 1072 and 104 in the bibliography just cited). As one pretty generally confirmed result may be mentioned, among others, that with the Ebbinghaus completion method girls are clearly inferior to boys of the same age.

one year to which 23 per cent. of the boys, but only 17 per cent. of the girls belong; the girls show a correspondingly greater percentage of their number at or above age.

TABLE VIII

SEX DIFFERENCES AS SHOWN BY BINET TESTS (GODDARD)

	Retarded			Advanced	
	Two Years or More	One Year	At Age	One Year	Two Years or More
Boys.......	18.5	23	34.5	20	4
Girls.......	18.5	17	36.5	23	5

Goddard's statement that retardation of marked amount is more frequent with boys is not borne out by his own tables, for the percentage of boys and girls is here the same, 18.5.[19]

All the other investigators that have treated the question of sex differences have obtained results more favorable for the boys.

Particularly decisive are the results obtained by Bloch and Preiss (38) upon *Volksschule* children in the manufacturing city of Kattowitz, in Upper Silesia. They tested 79 boys and 71 girls aged 7 to 11 years, all of whom displayed average native ability and average school ability. The percentages passing successfully the various tests show almost in every one of them a very decided inferiority of the girls. In Table IX I have brought together all the tests for which Bloch and Preiss report the results separately for the two sexes. No particular

[19]It must, of course, be borne in mind that these are pupils of schools for normal children, but the statement appears to be equally untrue for abnormal children. From one of Chotzen's tables (44, p. 462) I have calculated that excessive retardation, 5 years or more, appeared in 7 of 158 feeble-minded boys (4.5 per cent.), but in 11 of 122 girls (9 per cent.).

sex difference appears in the description of pictures and in the definition of abstract terms, and there is a slight superiority of the girls in the "hard" problem-questions; but in all the other tests the boys afford much higher percentages of success, often more than twice as high. Take, for instance, the 8-year old children: more than half of the boys, but not a single girl can arrange the five weights correctly; four-fifths of all 8-year old boys recall correctly what they have read, solve the easy problem-questions and state correctly the difference in things recalled in memory, whereas the percentage of girls

TABLE IX

SEX DIFFERENCES AS SHOWN BY BINET TESTS (BLOCH AND PREISS)

Test	Age	Percentage of Children Passing the Test — Boys	Girls
Description of Pictures	..	No difference	
Memory of Story Read	7	No difference	
	8	80	28
	9	No difference	
Arranging Three Weights	7	73	33
Arranging Five Weights	8	56	0
	9	66	29
	10	70	44
	11	77	42
Easy Problem-questions	8	81	55
	9	90	76
	10	100	100
Hard Problem-questions	9	25	41
	10	70	80
	11	70	80
Defining Abstract Terms	..	No difference	
Making a Sentence with Three Words	9	70	38
	10	82	40
	11	100	100
Arranging Words into Sentence	11	70	33
Naming 60 Words in 3 Minutes	..	76	50
Detecting Absurdities	11	77	40
Comparing Objects from Memory	7	60	50
	8	80	55

passing these tests successfully is only 28, 55 and 55, respectively. Where the same test runs through several years, the sex difference is nearly always greater in the younger than in the older children. This corresponds, again, with the psychological law that mental differences stand out more clearly in difficult than in easy tasks.

Bloch and Preiss themselves point out that the number of persons upon which these results are based is too small to warrant final conclusions, but it is surely worthy of note that the inferiority of the girls extends to so many different kinds of tests.

Bobertag (40, II, pp. 503-4) compared the same number of boys and girls of each age that ranked average in their school work. In each age the mental age of the boys turned out to be slightly above that of the girls; the difference amounted to 1/7 year in the 8, 9 and 12-year old pupils, and to 1/5 year in the 10 and 11-year old pupils.

Mlle. Descoeudres (46) compared a very small number of pupils—one intelligent and one unintelligent boy and a like pair of girls from each of six chronological ages. Taking all the right answers together, the boys had 52, the girls 48 per cent. There is here, then, also, a superiority of the boys, though the amount of the difference is not, of course, significant.

(*f*) *Repeated tests of the same children.* Attention must be called to one other important experiment included in the article of Bobertag's already mentioned (40, II)—an experiment that differs fundamentally from all that have been conducted heretofore. Bobertag retested in the year after a large number of the children (83 in all) that he had tested in 1909. The reapplication of the same tests does not seem to have caused any noticeable difficulty, because the memory of the details of the testing of the year before had as good as entirely disappeared. This experiment throws light upon three problems. In the first place it sheds an unexpectedly favorable light upon the *reliability* of the test method. Bobertag arranged the 83 children in order on the basis of the number of tests solved by each of them and found that the order in the two years coincided very closely, in fact the correlation amounted to 0.95. Accordingly, even if the absolute grading into the different age-levels of intelligence that the Binet-Simon method affords is still somewhat uncertain, yet it is demonstrably very certain in its *relative gradings*. The position that a child takes in a group of children on the basis of a single testing of his intelligence may be deemed to possess a high degree of reliability.

In the second place there comes to light a clear relation between the mental status of a child and the rate of his subsequent intellectual development. Those children that ranked 'at age' in the first testing had advanced next year exactly one year, on the average, while the retarded children had advanced only two-thirds of a year, and the advanced children one year and a quarter in the same period.

In the third place Bobertag found that the number of children that deviated, either above or below the level of their age, increased as their age increased. It follows from this that, as chronological age increases, the gradation of ages becomes progressively of less significance as a standard of variation: an intelligence that in the earlier years deviates above or below the level of its age by even less than a single year will in later years exceed this unit of deviation, which has then become relatively smaller. The same result had already been arrived at in investigating abnormal children, as will be shown in the following section.

4. *Abnormal Children*

(*a*) *Mental arrest and mental retardation. The mental quotient.* When Binet devised his system of tests, he had particularly in mind the testing of abnormal children in order that children of this type could be recognized opportunely and transferred to the special classes and to the institutions for the feeble-minded. Furthermore, Binet, together with Simon, tried out his method upon a large number of such children, though, unfortunately, he has given us no detailed account of this investigation, but he did draw conclusions from his experiments that express the relation of feeble-mindedness to his method in very simple formulas. One of these theses refers to mental retardation and runs thus (38, p. 113): "I am for my part of the opinion that every mental retardation amounting to two years can be regarded as a serious deficiency." A second of these theses refers to mental arrest and declares that the imbecile does not progress beyond the mental age of seven, the moron (feeble-minded in the narrower sense) beyond the mental age of nine.*

*By other investigators and elsewhere by Binet the upper limit of moronity is placed at 12 years.—*Translator.*

The second investigation of feeble-minded children, that of Goddard (47) likewise suffers from lack of sufficiently detailed data. Goddard tested the children and adults in the Institution for the Feeble-Minded at Vineland, N. J., nearly 400 persons in all, using the 1908 Binet series. He reports, however, only the frequency with which the several age-levels were reached and does not relate these data to the chronological ages of his subjects, so that it is quite impossible to determine the degree of retardation from his tables. We can only derive certain conclusions that will be mentioned later on.

The only thorough investigations that have thus far been made upon large numbers of abnormal children are, accordingly, the tests made at Breslau by the psychiatrist Kramer (54) and Chotzen (in conjunction with Nicolauer (43, 44)). These investigators, by testing children of different types, have supplemented each other's work in a fortunate manner. Kramer's material consisted partly of young persons who had been brought before the juvenile court and referred thence to the psychiatrist for expert opinion, partly of children that had visited the clinics on account of mental or nervous affections. Chotzen applied the tests in his capacity of city school medical inspector for special classes: he, therefore, tested all the children that were newly turned over to the special school for defectives. While Kramer had to do mostly with older children, Chotzen's business led him to deal mostly with children aged eight and nine years, but he extended his investigation by including some of the older children in the special school. The technique was patterned exactly after that followed by Bobertag, who had himself tested a group of abnormal children as well as normal children.

Both of these investigators express a favorable opinion of the value of the method for their purposes. Thus Kramer writes:

"In summing up our results we might say, first of all, that we are very much satisfied with the method for our purposes. Leaving the quantitative results entirely out of consideration, we came in the course of the testing, on account of the varied nature of the tests, to get acquainted with the peculiarities of the child's make-up, to understand surprisingly well his response to requirements of a varied sort, and acquired valuable insight into the qualitative differences in the method of reaction displayed by the feeble-minded. In the case of the children sent by the central office for corrective treatment, most of whom we could get hold of but for a single examination, the relatively short time that was needed (about 45 minutes to one hour) to reach a reliable judgment concerning their intelligence proved to be an exceptionally agreeable feature of the work. In all the cases in which a judgment concerning the intelligence could be reached by anamnestic data or on the basis of clinical observations themselves, there resulted with but few exceptions no contradictions with the outcome of the Binet testing" (54, p. 27).

To turn, now, to the figures: To begin with the second of the two theses of Binet that we cited above, his assertion of the existence of a "mental arrest" has also found confirmation in other directions. This thesis may be stated thus: *For every feeble-minded child there is a level which, once attained, represents a definite terminus for his capacities to meet the demands of mental tests.* That is, even though his age advances, his capacities do not advance further than this level.

Goddard found that the inmates of his institution were distributed in terms of mental age rather uniformly over the age-levels from one to nine years (with approximately 10 to 11 per cent. in each year), whereas the levels 10 to 12, taken together, comprised only 7 per cent. of the total number. Though here, again, he unfortunately put together those children whose age was such that they might perhaps have been able later to transcend the level in which they were then found and the other inmates whose development had for long been completely checked, yet his results do at least demonstrate that the feeble-minded only rarely transcend the mental age of nine.

By comparing these mental ages with the diagnoses of the physicians he arrived at the following schema:

		Imbeciles			
Type	Idiots	Low-grade	Middle-grade	High-grade	Morons
Mental ages....	1 to 2	3 to 4	5	6 to 7	8 to 12

Goddard's 'morons' coincide with our 'mentally feeble' (*Debilen*). The figures just given show that by far the greater number of them have a mental age of 8 and 9 years.

Kramer (54, p. 29) and Chotzen (44, p. 494) reached similar results.

Goddard compared the experimentally determined mental age with the general impression that the children had made on the teachers and officers of the institution and found a very satisfying amount of agreement. The children of a given mental age formed a fairly homogeneous group, both in respect to their every-day accomplishments and their ability to adapt themselves to the demands of institutional life. He adds to this a description of what can be expected in the line of practical behavior of a child of a given mental age. But all of these statements stand very much in need of further testing.

It is well to give here explicit warning against a certain false conception of the term "arrest." An imbecile who, during his life, never progresses past the mental age of seven, is not on that account to be thought of as the same as a seven-year old child. He does grow beyond that status in many respects: he acquires experiences that a normal 7-year old child does not possess, picks up many accomplishments, experiences the awakening within himself of impulses and needs that come with increasing years. The arrest, then, pertains only to that specific group of mental abilities that are tested by the tests. And even some ones of these abilities may show some development (cf. in this connection p. 86), only there still remain so many defects of a fundamental nature that, all in all, it is impossible for him to rise above the mental age of seven.

Of importance is, furthermore, the discovery that Goddard made concerning the mental age of a special group, the *morally feeble-minded.* It turned out that this group was recruited solely from the upper of the age-levels represented in the institution. Of 22 such individuals, 15 had the mental age 9, 5 the age 10 and one each the ages 11 and 12. The circumstance that moral defects do not extend down beyond the mental age nine is explained by Goddard in the following way: Certain immoral instincts, like the impulse to lie, to steal, etc., normally awaken about the ninth year; later on reasoning develops and puts these tendencies under inhibition. With children whose mental age is below nine those instincts are not yet developed, whereas with children who are arrested at about the mental age of nine, the instincts do show themselves without getting far enough along to develop the inhibition and so become a moral defect.

We may leave undecided the question of the correctness of this explanation, but in any event the fact remains that *pronounced retardation in morality is not associated with equally pronounced intellectual deficiency.* The moral deficiency therefore displays a certain independence in its existence, and to that extent the old designation "moral insanity" was not utterly devoid of significance.

We may allude, also, at this point, to a very similar conclusion reached by Kramer, who must, naturally, have encountered this type frequently among his criminal subjects. He says: "We have to do here with individuals whose defectiveness is on the moral side and in whom there can be noted even from their early youth a decided lack of moral ideas and altruistic spirit. In raising the question as to in how far these moral defects exist independent of intellectual deficiency, it is worth noting that in the examination a number of these children obtained a result that corresponded with their actual age. And even in the cases in which the mental ability fell below the norm, there was no parallelism at all between the two kinds of deficiency."[20]

---

[20]See Reference 54, p. 28. We may mention also in this connection the results obtained by Frau Dosai-Révész (4) with separate tests. She compared the efficiency in computation, memory and report of normal children, simple feeble-minded and morally feeble-minded and found that the results for the last-named group fell almost entirely between the results for the two other groups.

But this discussion has already led us from the consideration of mental arrest to the question of *the mental retardation of the feeble-minded.* Binet used as the measure of retardation simply the difference between mental age and chronological age and was so convinced of the general application of this measure that he looked upon the value "2 years" as a general expression for a definite and in fact serious deficiency.

Binet's successors also made use of this standard, but their own results teach us that we can not be satisfied with it. For it has become evident that *one and the same absolute difference, e. g., a mental retardation of three years, means very different things at different years.* Thus Kramer (54) remarks: "It should not be concluded that a 12-year old child with a mental age of 9 is of the same degree of feeble-mindedness as an 8-year[21] child with a mental age of 5. In the case of the children turned over to us for examination by the Central Child Welfare Bureau (*Jugendfürsorgezentrale*) it came out clearly that the differences revealed among the younger children were for the most part but small, but among the older children always greater, although the actual defects in these two groups, so far as we could judge them by other criteria, by no means revealed any corresponding difference, but seemed, on the average, to be about the same." Chotzen (44, p. 493) also corroborates this view: "On account of a checking of development, the mental age

[21]Page 29. In the text there is a typographical error here, 7 instead of 8-year.

of feeble-minded children lags progressively more and more behind their chronological age: the younger they are, the more, and the older they are, the less does a year's retardation mean in actual defectiveness."

How considerable the fluctuations are may be shown by some figures (Table X) that I have derived from one of Chotzen's tables (p. 485). In addition to the tests, or rather independently of them, Chotzen examined all the pupils of the special school as the physician and the psychiatrist ordinarily would, and classified them, on the basis of this examination, into the stock groups—moron, imbecile, idiot. Some he had to class outside of these groups by designating them as 'not feeble-minded' or as 'doubtful feeble-minded.' Now, it might be supposed that the members of any group, *e. g.*, the morons, would necessarily show at least approximately the same degree of mental endowment, regardless of differences in their chronological ages. But Table X shows that their mental retardation, computed as the absolute difference, has very different values with the older than with the younger children, and Table XI, in which the average value of this measure of retardation has been figured for each age-level, reveals a rapid increase in the magnitude of the value, so that the 12-year-old imbeciles are retarded by twice as many years as the 8-year-old imbeciles (4.7 as against 2.3 years).

From this it seems to me to follow that the absolute difference can be used only when we are dealing with children of a given age. If, for example, it should sometime be arranged to carry out tests of intelligence upon all 6-year-old children when they entered school, then the designations "retarded one year" or "advanced one year" would have an unequivocal meaning.

TABLE X

FREQUENCY OF MENTAL RETARDATION IN DIFFERENT FORMS OF FEEBLE-MINDEDNESS AND DIFFERENT CHRONOLOGICAL AGES

	Not Feeble-minded				Doubtfully Defective			
Retardation.....	0	1 Yr.	2 Yrs.	3 Yrs.	1 Yr.	2 Yrs.	3 Yrs.	4 Yrs.
Chronological Age. 8	6	11			13	4		
9		7	5		1	3		
10			2			3		
11				1			1	1
12			1				1	
13							1	1

	Morons				Imbeciles				
Retardation........	1 Yr.	2 Yrs.	3 Yrs.	4 Yrs.	1 Yr.	2 Yrs.	3 Yrs.	4 Yrs.	5 Yrs.
Chronological Age......... 8	4	10	2		6	21	9	2	1
9		15	2			8	30	8	2
10		5	7				7	5	4
11			5	1				2	
12			2	1				1	2

But it is another matter when we have to consider children of quite different ages or when we want to express the degree of backwardness in a formula of general validity. The value based on absolute difference, if given by itself, may mean very different things, so that at least the chronological age ought always to be stated to enable the reader to figure out the degree of importance to be attached to the difference. To what prolixity of statement this method leads one may be illustrated by the following sentence from Chotzen (pp. 493-4): "Children of 8 to 9 years can suffer a deficiency of one year, those of 10 to 12 years one of two years without feeble-mindedness being present, but a backwardness of two, or of three years, respectively, for these ages, certainly cannot coexist with normal intelligence."

TABLE XI

AVERAGE RETARDATION, IN YEARS, OF THE CHILDREN IN TABLE X

Chronological Age	Not Feeble-minded	Doubtful Defect	Morons	Imbeciles
8	0.65	1.3	1.9	2.3
9	1.4	1.7	2.1	3.1
10	2.0	2.0	2.6	3.8
11	3.0	3.5	3.2	4.0
12	2.0	3.0	3.3	4.7
13		3.5		

That the size of the absolute difference for the same degree of feeble-mindedness should increase as age increases is psychologically easily intelligible, for, since feeble-mindedness consists essentially in a condition of development that is below the normal condition, the *rate* of development will also be a slower one, and thus every added year of age must magnify the difference in question, at least as long as there is present anything that could be called mental development at all. With this in mind it is but a step to the idea of measuring the backwardness by the relative difference, *i. e.*, by the ratio between mental and chronological age, instead of by the absolute difference. Bobertag had already conceived a plan of this sort, while Kramer (54, p. 30) hints at something of the sort, though very guardedly: "Whether perhaps there might be devised a specific method of calculation for relating the difference in years to chronological age and which would then give us an absolute measure for degree of feeble-mindedness, seems to me a matter of doubt."

The results of Chotzen that now lie before us permit us to test the feasibility of a relative measure of this sort. I should like to recommend the relating to chronological age not of the difference, but of the mental age itself. We would then obtain the *mental quotient* that has already been mentioned (p. 42). *This quotient shows what fractional part of the intelligence normal to his age a feeble-minded child attains. Mental quotient = mental age ÷ chronological age.* An 8-year old child with a mental age of six has, then, a mental quotient of 6/8 = 0.75. A 12-year old child with a mental age of 9 has the same mental quotient.

TABLE XII

AVERAGE MENTAL QUOTIENT OF THE CHILDREN IN TABLES X AND XI

Chronological Age	Not Feeble-minded	Doubtful Defect	Morons	Imbeciles
8	0.92	0.84	0.76	0.71
9	0.85	0.81	0.77	0.67
10	(0.80)	(0.80)	0.74	0.62
11	(0.73)	(0.68)	0.71	(0.64)
12	(0.75)	(0.75)	(0.73)	(0.61)
13		(0.73)		

Now when we turn into quotients the values calculated from Chotzen in Table XI, we obtain Table XII. The idiots have been omitted for reasons that will appear later. The figures in brackets are those that cannot be deemed reliable averages on account of too few individuals included in them. The table reveals mental quotients for the two main forms of feeble-mindedness that are, it is true, not constant, but that are, however, very similar through several chronological years. The morons, in especial, show surprisingly uniform values; their average quotient varies only within the narrow range 0.71 to 0.77 for the five years 8 to 12. Roughly expressed, therefore, their intelligence, measured by that of normal persons, is a 'three-quarter intelligence.' The imbeciles show somewhat greater variations, but their mental quotients are in quite fair agreement, at least for the years 9 to 11. They entitle their possessors, again roughly speaking, to a scant 'two-thirds intelligence.'

The first two of Chotzen's groups are represented by too few cases to permit consideration of their averages, save at most for the younger ages. In these ages the mental quotient agrees finely with the medical diagnosis of the children. Those designated as "not feeble-minded" have a mental quotient of about 0.90, while the doubtfully-defective, whose quotient lies between 0.80 and 0.84, form a real intermediate grade between the 'not-abnormal' and the true morons. The isolated cases of older children (7 in all) that Chotzen classified in these two groups, are ranked by their quotient largely in the morons. It is possible that the mental quotient may supplement uncertain medical diagnoses in cases of this sort.

Now the objection might be raised to the above series of quotients that they comprise only averages and that these have been derived in part from a too small number of values. To meet this objection I have made another computation in which I have worked out the mental quotients of *individual children*, and then have recorded their frequency-distribution. In this computation I have disregarded chronological age, and have combined in each case the values for 10 points on the scale, *e. g.*, the quotients lying between 1.00 and 91, between 0.81 and 0.90, etc.

TABLE XIII

DISTRIBUTION OF MENTAL QUOTIENTS IN DIFFERENT GROUPS OF FEEBLE-MINDED

Mental Quotient	Not Feeble-Md'd Abs.	Not Feeble-Md'd Rel.	Doubtful Abs.	Doubtful Rel.	Morons Abs.	Morons Rel.	Imbeciles Abs.	Imbeciles Rel.
0.91-1.00....	6	18						
0.81-0.90....	19	57	14	48	5	9	6	5.5
0.71-0.80....	8	25	13	45	37	67	30	27.
0.61-0.70....			2	7	13	24	49	44.
0.51-0.60....							15	13.5
0.41-0.50....							9	8
0.31-0.40....							2	2
Totals...	33	100	29	100	55	100	111	100

Table XIII shows the distribution of the results obtained in this way, both in absolute numbers and in percentages: Figure 1 also shows the distribution of the percentages graphically.

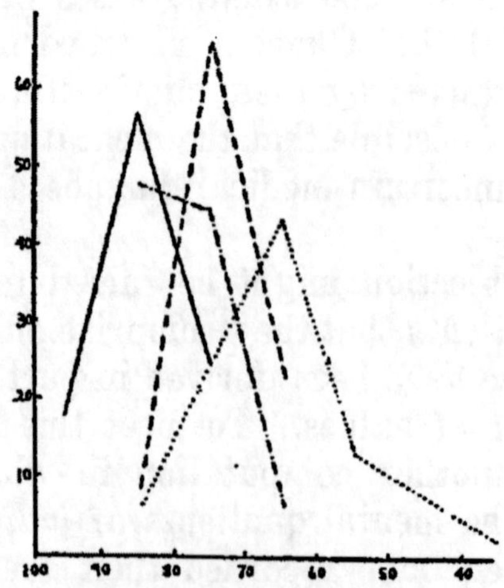

FIG. 1. DISTRIBUTION OF MENTAL QUOTIENTS DERIVED FROM CHOTZEN'S RESULTS.

———————— = not feeble-minded.
— — — — — — = doubtful.
—.—.—.—.—.—. = moron.
.... = imbecile.

There appears a clear separation of the points of maximal frequency for the chief groups, and, it is to be noted, the mental quotient of the 'not-abnormal' children lies mostly between 0.81 and 0.90, that of the morons between 0.71 and 0.80, that of the imbeciles between 0.61 and 0.70—all quite in accordance with our earlier figures. In the case of the imbeciles the range of the quotients is wider than with the other groups, as the average values had already shown. Attention should be called to the fairly symmetrical form of the three curves: this brings it about that the point of maximal frequency and the average tend to coincide within each group.

The transitional character of the group of doubtfully defective also finds expression typically in that its members are distributed fairly uniformly over the regions that are characteristic on the one hand of the normals and on the other hand of the undoubted morons.

The number of the children tested by Chotzen is not yet large enough and particularly their distribution over the different age-levels is not wide enough to consider the above figures as having conclusive value for other sets of material, yet they do seem to me so far removed from objection as to demonstrate that the mental quotient is a very much more useful measure of backwardness than the commonly used absolute difference.

The quotient does not seem, however, to afford an actually constant expression of degree of feeblemindedness, but shows a tendency to fall in value as age increases. This tendency, it is evident, is but slight within the limits of age that have been mentioned, so that for many problems it can be neglected. Before and after these ages the fall in the value seems to take place more rapidly. In the case of the later age-levels this is easily intelligible, for once the stage of arrest that we have previously discussed is reached (for morons at the mental age of 9), the quotient obtained by dividing mental by chronological age must decrease as chronological age increases. The feeble-minded child, it must be remembered, not only has a slower rate of development than the normal child, but also reaches a stage of arrest at an age when the normal child's intelligence is still pushing forward in its development. At this time, then, the cleft between the two will be markedly widened.

From these considerations it follows that the mental quotient can hold good as an index of feeble-mindedness only during that period when the development of the feeble-minded individual is still in progress. It is for this reason that there is no sense in calculating the quotient for idiots, because, in their case, the stage of arrested development has been entered upon long before the ages at which they are being subjected to examination. The above-mentioned gradual tendency of the mental quotient to sink during the progress of development shows that this development approaches the final level of arrest at a progressively decreasing rate.[22]

Whether we shall succeed some time in finding a formula for a truely constant coefficient of feeble-mindedness must be left for the future.

---

[22]In his last article (40, II) Bobertag lays special stress on this progressive retardation in the rate of development of the feeble-minded and attempts to present it in graphic form.

(*b*) *Relation to the several tests.* It must not be thought that the significance of the Binet-Simon method for the study of feeble-mindedness is restricted to the possibility of grading them quantitatively. Perhaps even more important than this is the *qualitative analysis* of the individual subject that the method allows and the discovery of how the several tests have participated in the final values. Chotzen's investigation, the first to attack this problem, has shown how confusingly many special problems and matters of interest are to be unearthed in this field.

At the very outset, for example, there is thrust insistently upon us the question: Have we any right at all to equate a 10-year-old feeble-minded child with a 7-year-old normal child just because the result of testing gives him a mental age of 7 years: in other words, can we say that feeble-mindedness is actually mere 'backwardness.' It is, indeed, quite often asserted that this expression is misleading because feeble-mindedness is something qualitatively different from normality. But the Binet-Simon method makes it possible for us to work out the comparison between the two mental conditions exactly.

And in fact comparison does show that the mental age of 7 years is not reached in the tests in quite the same way that the normal 7-year-old child reaches the same mental age, for *the area of irregular distribution is very much wider with the feeble-minded than with the normal child*. Bobertag, in an as yet unpublished discussion, reckons the distribution at twice the area of that of a normal child. In other words we may say that the 'hits' and 'misses' of the older feeble-minded children are scattered over very many more age-levels than are those of younger normal children: the defective fails unexpectedly to pass some quite easy tests, but succeeds here and there in meeting much higher requirements. There appears a certain dissociation of abilities that are normally more strictly intercorrelated.

We are now in a position, moreover, to discover a general principle obtaining in this dissociation. *There are certain abilities that are essentially a function of age, relatively independent of intelligence: there are other abilities that are conditioned entirely by specific degrees of intellectual development, regardless of the age at which this development is attained.* A child of 9 or 10 years of age, even if he be defective, will be farther advanced than a normal child of 6 or 7 years of age in abilities of the first sort; but a normal child necessarily surpasses a feeble-minded child in abilities of the second sort.

A priori we should expect that to the first sort of abilities (those conditioned by age) would belong those dependent upon a mass of experiences frequently had and activities frequently discharged in everyday life. But *a priori* opinions of this sort are of no great service to us, and it will be of correspondingly great value for us to be able to discover by an analysis of the results of Binet-Simon tests which of the tests applied to the feeble-minded correlate more with age and which more with real intelligence. Up to now the results of Chotzen are alone available for this purpose and even they afford but an incomplete survey because Chotzen had to deal almost entirely with feeble-minded children of a single age-group (8 to 9 years).

Chotzen gives us a whole series of computations to show the worth of the different tests for the diagnosis of feeble-mindedness: the perusal of his difficult exposition will afford the reader a new idea of the complications that arise when one really tries to analyze the serial system of tests to the last details. Because a repetition of investigations of this sort, especially with feeble-minded children of more advanced ages is very much to be desired, we feel warranted in introducing here a brief account of the methods that Chotzen pursued in evaluating the tests.

The simplest thing is, of course, the direct comparison of feeble-minded with normal children of the same age (using Bobertag's data).

From such a comparison it appeared (44, p. 440) that the backwardness of the feeble-minded was *least* in the following tests: telling forenoon from afternoon, defining in terms of use, knowing own age, esthetic judgment, telling the number of the fingers, describing a picture, counting 13 pennies; the backwardness was, on the other hand, *very pronounced* in the following: memory-span for 16 syllables and for 5 digits, making change (80 *Pfennige* for 1 *Mark*), counting backward from 20 to 0, definition by superordinate terms, comparison of two objects from memory, recall of a short story, naming the months and arranging the five weights.

With children of other ages these lists would presumably change. Thus the explanation of the picture which is demanded of older children would doubtless bring out a decided difference between normal and feeble-minded children, though the description of the picture which is demanded of the younger children did not bring out such a difference, according to Chotzen.

However, even these lists of Chotzen's suffice to show that the differences between the two types of children turn out to be small in those tests that relate to frequently practiced activities (counting, telling how old they are) and to common experiences of everyday life (number of fingers, forenoon and afternoon); on the other hand, the deficiency of the feeble-minded is at once revealed in its entirety the moment that something unusual is demanded, that something new is presented and that attention must be sharply concentrated.

A similar comparison can be carried out, in the next place, amongst the special-class pupils themselves, *i. e.*, between the different groups of feebleminded that the medical diagnosis had established: Chotzen found out which tests exhibited a specially decided drop from one group to another in the feeble-minded children of the same age. I mention only those that showed a clear falling off of one-half in passing from the "not feeble-minded" to the morons and from the morons to the imbeciles.

For 8- and 9-year-old children: drawing a diamond, repeating five digits, easy problem-questions. There was a somewhat smaller falling off in counting five coins and comparing two objects.

For older children (Chotzen had also tested a series of older children for purposes of comparison): comparison, reproduction of the item in the newspaper, arranging five weights, making change, defining by superordinate terms, knowing various pieces of money, repeating five digits.

Thirdly and lastly, Chotzen figured out comparative results for those subjects of the same mental, but of different chronological age, as might happen, for instance, if an 8-year-old child were retarded two years, a 9-year-old child three years, or a 10-

year old child four years. He found that when children of a single mental level were considered, some tests show a clear increase in capacity with increase in chronological age, others no alteration, while yet others an actual decrease. Tests of the first sort, those that have an 'age-increase,' are doubtless tests that have least to do with intelligence, because, given the same intelligence, they are nevertheless better done by the older children. On the contrary, the other tests plainly stand in correlation with intelligence, more particularly the tests in which the older children actually turn out poorer. The following are the results:

Decided increase with age is shown in copying, writing from dictation, the recall of two items of a story, naming the days of the week.

"The tests accompanied by strong increase with age relate, then, almost exclusively to matters of information, particularly of school-information, the assimilation of which depends on the extent of instruction. Where only a slight increase is to be detected, information also plays a rôle in some of the tests (five coins, knowing age), but for the most part the tests are such that not only practise, but also the natural increase of efficiency will improve the results, *e. g.*, execution of three orders, counting backwards, repeating 16 syllables. In all of these the increase with age is slight. No increase at all is present with tests that demand ability to judge and to combine or with such as put severe demands upon apprehension—comparison, problem-questions, noting omissions, repeating five digits" (44, p. 453).

To this last category probably belong also: recall of six details of a story, arrangement of the five weights, explanation of a picture, making change, though the figures are too small in these cases to permit positive conclusions.

When we compare with each other these different lists obtained in different ways, we note, it is true, deviations in many details, yet, taken as a whole, the same tests keep cropping up as the ones in which defective intelligence is laid bare, unconcealed and uncompensated, while in the other tests the defect of intelligence can be made good by greater age.

When investigations of this kind shall have been carried out with a large number of feeble-minded individuals of different chronological ages, we may hope to reach a far deeper insight into the whole structure of defective intelligence in its different stages of development and degrees of enfeeblement.

(*c*) *Intelligence and school ability.* The problem we have already met with the normal children (pp. 57 ff.) meets us again with the abnormal and leads us to quite similar conclusions. That is, only a partial correspondence exists between the magnitude of the mental defect and the reduction in school ability. Kramer states that a large number of children were retarded in their school classes by the same number of years as they were retarded in intelligence, yet there were a good many who were more backward in school status than in intelligence (the opposite condition, less backward in the school, almost never obtained). In fact, there were some children completely incompetent for school work in whom no corresponding mental defect could be made out.

Similarly, among the 8- and 9-year-old children turned over to the special classes (auxiliary school) Chotzen found a large number that did not have the two years of backwardness demanded by Binet for such a condition, but who, nevertheless, certainly belonged in the special school, because they failed completely in the regular school.

This pedagogical retardation that is non-intellectually conditioned is, as will be understood, in some cases a product of external conditions, in particular of poor home conditions, neglect, change of residence and school, long illness, etc. In other cases, however, what is lacking is something internal: those *volitional* attributes that must supplement intelligence to produce useful men are not developed to the same degree as the intelligence. There are, then, the morally feeble-minded: "children of this type, as one might expect, shirk their lessons, are up to all sorts of mischief in the class, are quite unaffected by punishments, and so forth, so that, despite good intelligence, they more or less often fail of promotion. Those cases in which these mental anomalies are accompanied by intellectual deficiency of a small degree prove to be especially unpropitious (Kramer, 54, p. 31).

5. *Points of View for the Reorganization and Improvement of the Gradation Method*

Our discussion has revealed already a series of more or less serious defects in the Binet-Simon method, nor have these defects been removed by the revision made by Binet himself in 1911. Nearly every user of the method has called attention to weaknesses of some sort in it; moreover, many do more than merely criticize; they make proposals for modifying or supplementing the method, or even make use themselves without more ado of modified methods of conducting the tests at this or that point.

But it would become a very serious matter if individual investigators, on mere grounds of personal preference or chance bits of criticism, should be forever making changes in an instrument of investigation that has attained international usage; on the one hand such tinkering will destroy the balance of the whole system in which every test is peculiarly bound up with every other test, and on the other hand it will put an end to the comparison of the results of different investigators.

For these reasons it is to be recommended that we proceed in the future in this way: wherever our object is to lay the emphasis on the substance of the results secured, as in the testing of children for practical purposes, let us for the present still continue to use the old system, despite its evident defects. But independently from this, let investigations directed to methodological issues be undertaken *with the aim of constructing a gradation system that shall be revised in every particular.* But this task is beyond the ability of the individual investigator: the problems to be solved are too many and varied and the number of individuals that should be tested is too great. Rather is it true that here, if anywhere, is there opportunity for that community and division of work that is everywhere now demanded in psychology.

To prepare the way for the carrying out of such a program I enumerate here the chief points to be considered in this work of reconstruction and also offer for discussion some specific proposals of my own for modifications in the system.

(*a*) *Selection and appraisement of the various tests.* The criticism that has been passed upon the various tests has been based sometimes on theoretical considerations, sometimes on practical results. The critique of Ayres (31), who has done no work himself with the method, is an instance of the first type. He complains that the tests have too seldom a direct relation to *practical* intelligence, that they principally concern such things as fluent use of language, memory span, response to problem questions that are quite foreign to real life, and also in part attainments that are to a great degree dependent on instruction and on influences of the home environment, and also work with abstract concepts—something, he says, with which only philosophers have to deal (!), whereas they do not touch the ability to get on with the activities of life; he wants more "doing tests" introduced. Although Ayres' criticism is justified in many respects, yet he seems to have overlooked the fundamental fact that intelligence is a formal activity, and that of necessity it is operative also in tasks whose content is not such as appears in real life. Indeed, problems of this sort have the methodological advantage that there is certainly no uncontrollable influence of training in them.

More important are the criticisms that proceed from the empirical retrial of the tests. It has been shown that, as a matter of fact, there is too intimate dependence with school and environmental influences in many of the tests; others could not be assigned positively to a specific age-level or showed no clear differences in the performances of children of unmistakably different intelligence. Again, objection is to be raised to those tests in which there is a strong probability that the right answer may be a matter of mere chance, like the tests: "Show me your right hand, your left ear" and "Is it forenoon or afternoon?"

The fitness of a test to be employed at all, and its assignment to a given age-level is something that we shall be able in the future to work out by different methods.

In the first place we have to make use of the relation between the age-level and the test. In general, for a test to be valid for a certain level, the requirement is that approximately 75 per cent. of all children of this age shall be able to pass the test. This requirement would correspond to the normal standard of validity previously mentioned (p. 45 f.), and Bobertag, as more recently Bell (32), has actually checked up the assignment of given tests to given age-levels in accordance with this principle; Terman and Childs (63) take 66 per cent. for the critical value, though this would seem, for the reasons already cited, to be less appropriate.

Taken alone, however, this principle is inadequate, for it does not inform us whether the test would be characteristic for just this age-level *only* and not just as much or nearly as much for another age-level. To determine this we must discover with what frequency the test is passed in other ages; and *that test is most useful that shows the most decided advance with age* (a helpful methodological device to which Bobertag was the first to call attention).

For the sake of illustration let us invent an example. Suppose two tests have each been passed successfully by 75 per cent. of 9-year-old children, but that the one test shows little, the other decided difference in the frequency with which it is passed by 8- and 10-year old children. If Test A be passed by 65, 75 and 80 per cent. of 8-, 9- and 10-year old children, respectively, and Test B by 45, 75 and 90 per cent. in the same three ages, respectively, then the latter test sets a task whose performance is just normal for the 9-year-old, as compared with the 8-year-old children, and practically a self-evident activity for 10-year-old children; Test B is then the more useful test.

Since the process of mental development brings into maturity in succession a series of different part-functions, it follows that for each age there should be a series of tests to correspond to the phenomena of development that have just appeared; it must be possible, with the aid of the principle of decided advance with age, to pick these tests out from a number of others.

Again, the matter of *correspondence between the results of different investigations* must be considered in the selection of the tests. A test that grades the same or nearly the same with German, French, English and American children has naturally more claim to be included in the final system than one that varies markedly with the examiner or with the examinees. The table that Bell (32) has prepared is instructive in this connection. He presents, side by side, the age-rank that each of the Binet-Simon tests would have attained on the basis of the results of Binet, Levistre and Morlé, Johnstone, Goddard, Bobertag, and Terman and Childs.[23]

In many of the tests the variations are quite large; thus, the test of "comparing two objects from memory" ranges from the 6th year (Johnstone) to the 9th year (Terman and Childs), the test of "naming 60 words in three minutes" from the 10th year (Goddard) to the 15th year (Levistre and Morlé, Terman and Childs). The assignment of such a test to a single age-level becomes, then, evidently an arbitrary matter. Over against these are other tests that show great constancy, at least so far. Thus, "counting 13 pennies," "esthetic comparison," "showing right hand and left

---

[23]It must be remembered that the tables and materials from which Bell had to construct his summary have been assembled so differently by the different investigators that their gauging of the several tests is not really directly comparable, so that Bell's tables must be regarded merely as a preliminary attempt at checking up the results of various investigations.

ear" fluctuate in rank-assignment only between the 6th and the 7th years, the "recognition of omissions in drawings" only between the 7th and the 8th years, the test of "counting backward from 20" only between the 8th and the 9th year, that of "naming the months" only between the 9th and the 10th year. The "hard problem-questions" test is ranked by all these investigators save Goddard in the 12th year, etc.

It will be seen that these are for the most part tests in which verbal formulation plays little or no part. It is, indeed, quite natural that where the problem and its answer are intimately connected with verbal expression, national peculiarities must make themselves evident; but it will be possible to reduce this source of error if more heed is given in the future to the transference of the tests from the one language to the other in such a way as to fit as exactly as possible the linguistic and cultural tone of the second nation and thus secure equal difficulty in the problems: the actual verbal translation that has been used by many investigators has often failed to meet this requirement. Thus, for instance, the rather free adaptation of the method that Bobertag made for Germany has yielded in many cases results in closer accord with those of Binet than have the literal translations of the Americans.

Finally, we shall have also to judge the value of a test according as it does succeed in bringing plainly to light *differences in intelligence* that are known from other sources to exist. On this point Mlle. Descoeudres (46) has carried out a study of the present Binet tests, though, to be sure, upon but a limited number of children. She tested one "intelligent" and one "unintelligent" child from each of the six years of a boys' and of a girls' *Volksschule:* the selection was determined by the teachers' estimates of the pupils' intelligence. When, now, she compared the results of the tests for the 12 unintelligent and the 12 intelligent children, taken as groups, she found that the differentiation of the two groups appeared with quite unequal clearness in the different tests. Those tests in which the intelligent had the clearest advantage over the unintelligent (and that therefore have the most claim for consideration as tests of intelligence) are cited in the first column of Table XIV.

TABLE XIV

BINET TESTS WHEREIN A CLEAR DIFFERENCE IS SHOWN

Between Intelligent and Unintelligent Normal Children (Descoeudres).	Between Normal and Feeble-Minded Children (Chotzen).	Between Different Grades of Feeble-Minded Children (Descoeudres).
Arranging 5 weights. *Definition superior to use.* *Counting backward.* *Explanation of picture.* Noting omissions in drawings. Detecting absurdities.	*Arranging 5 weights.* *Definition superior to use.* *Counting backward.* *Comparison of two objects from memory.* Repeating five digits, 16 syllables, and the story. Counting coins. Making change.	*Definitions.* *Description of picture.* *Comparison of two objects from memory.* Problem-questions.

Mlle. Descoeudres has also undertaken a study of feeble-minded children (73), which may be introduced here for comparison. (We shall have occasion to discuss it in more detail later in another connection.) The children were arranged in order of the estimated degree of their feeble-mindedness and with this was compared their capacity in 15 different tests. Among these tests were six from the Binet-Simon series, four of which yielded extraordinarily high correlations (between 0.80 and 0.88) with the estimated intelligence. These four tests are listed in the third column of Table XIV. With the tests of "knowing coins" and "naming of 60 words in three minutes" the correspondence was of lesser degree.

And thirdly, we must call to mind the results of Chotzen to which we have already referred (p. 87), in which certain tests gave far clearer expression than others to the difference between normal and feeble-minded children of the same age. These tests are listed in the second column of the table.

It is worth noting that most of the tests appear several times in the three columns, despite the fact that the three investigations were carried out with children of quite different ages and under otherwise varying conditions. This shows that certain tests are particularly fitted to bring differences in intelligence out in clear relief, and at the same time it shows us a way to pick out these true tests of intelligence from the rest.[24]

It is unnecessary to add that there is no reason why controls like these should be limited only to the tests already used by Binet; in fact, comparisons between intelligent and unintelligent pupils have already been carried out for the most varied sorts of tests by Meumann, Winteler, Cohn-Dieffenbacher and many foreign investigators. From these and other future investigations like them there will surely

[24]There is one other point of correspondence that ought to be mentioned, viz., that the differentiation of the children according to their social status was also revealed for the greater part by these same characteristic tests as revealed the intellectual differentiation (see pp. 53f.).

be found certain tests of so decided a symptomatic value that they will deserve to be adapted for introduction into the graded system. In this connection we may allude among others to the modifications of the Masselon test recently proposed by Meumann (v. p. 16)—a test that Meumann believes is usually solved with logical insight by the intelligent but not so by the unintelligent.

Investigations in correlational psychology of which we shall speak in the next section likewise afford many tests whose results exhibit decided correspondence with estimated intelligence. These tests are evidently not such as can be introduced directly into the system of graded tests because they deal with fine gradation, whereas the Binet scale recognizes only tests that present merely the alternatives "right" or "wrong." Possibly, however, they will admit of rearrangement into a simpler form appropriate to the scale.

By using all the methodological resources that we have cited we shall gradually succeed in selecting tests that are far more characteristic of the intelligence of a given age-level than those now in use and that are homogeneous for the different cultural groups and nations to be tested.

(*b*) *The composition of series for the several years.* Since intelligence is a formal capacity that can be determined only by multiform testing, care must be taken that each single age-level should have a manifold of tests. It is not enough, therefore, to put together any sort of separate tests that happen to be passed by 75 per cent. of those of the age-level in question. If the tests are too similar to one another, their combination does little more that the testing by any one of them would do. Binet and Simon did not keep this principle sufficiently in mind: some of their age-levels contain only linguistic tests and no tests of activity.

Furthermore, the age-levels, considered as wholes, must also be adjusted, for to demand that particular tests be passed and to demand that all five tests of a given age-level shall be passed are two entirely different things. This adjustment is rendered more difficult by the fact that in computing mental age one must not only deal with the tests of one age-level, but also make supplementary use of tests from the higher levels; accordingly, in this adjustment of the levels as a whole attention must be paid to the interrelation of tests that come into consideration in connection with different near-by age-levels.

The controlling principle for the adjustment or standardization of the age-levels is that approximately symmetrical distribution of the mental ages must prevail for each level. That is, the tests are properly arranged and skillfully assembled into a system if, when a large number of unselected normal children of a given age are tested, a large middle group stand 'at age' and the rest are divided fairly equally between advanced and retarded cases.

To carry out such investigations practically it will be necessary to try as many tests as possible with each pupil; in this way it will be feasible to assign the passing of each particular test to this or that age-level and to discover the general arrangement of the tests that furnishes the closest to a symmetrical distribution.

The investigation can be made with more precision if the curve of distribution be based upon the mental quotient instead of the mental age, for we should then anticipate fairly good correspondence between the curves of distribution of the different age-levels. The mental quotients for each age-level would then be grouped together in 10 per cent. ranges, *i. e.*, we should have first the children with mental quotients ranging from 0.91 to 1.00 and 1.00 to 1.10 that would form the compact middle group, then on either side of them groups of rapidly diminishing frequencies, those with mental quotients .81 to .90, .71 to .80, etc., below, and those with quotients 1.11 to 1.20, 1.21 to 1.30, etc., above.

In the older form of the Binet-Simon scale the number of tests assigned to each year differed. In 1911 Binet put five tests in every age; it is to be recommended that this idea of uniformity be followed in the future because the computation of the final status is much simplified in that way.[25]

(*c*) *The extension of the system.* In the next place the system of tests is to be extended beyond its present limits and in different directions.

Thus far the lack of tests has been most seriously felt in the upper years. The tests that Binet and others have devised above the 11th year have been thus far quite tentative and provisional; at the best they could furnish us the necessary supplementary material for the ascertainment of mental ages 10 and 11, but they absolutely fail to provide a direct

[25] Cf. also the provisional new arrangement of Bobertag in Appendix II.

measurement for the mental ages 12 to 15. We must admit that the discovery of appropriate tests for these higher levels of mental maturity is much more difficult than for the younger children, but the difficulty is to be overcome. Thus, Terman and Childs (64) have recently proposed a series of tests, each one of which is susceptible to diverse gradings with respect to the capacities that it requires, so that it can be employed up to mental age 15. Among these tests are arithmetical reasoning, familiarity with a list of selected words, a generalization test (discovering the 'moral' of a fable that is read to the subject) and the Ebbinghaus completion test with the task made progressively more difficult.[26]

Let us hope that in such a way we may gradually advance from one year to another and may finally create a series for adults as the termination of the whole scale. However, this problem is certainly not so easy of solution as Binet thought when he transferred to higher ages tests that he had originally developed for the years 11, 12 and 13, and made the last of these groups over into tests for "adults" by the addition of two new ones.

Another thing that is greatly to be desired is an extension of the system by the creation of *parallel series of tests for* each year.[27] How gladly would we use the method to trace the mental development of the same children through several years; but there are difficulties in the way of this, because, of course, when the same tests are repeated, the child

[26] See Appendix II.

[27] Cf. Binet, 36, p. 163.

confronts them with a different attitude.[28] But if we had at our disposal other equivalent series of tests, it would be possible to make repeated testings of the same individuals more frequently. In the same way, when group tests were carried on, those children between whom there might be danger of collusion could be tested with different series. Finally, it is valuable to have a supplementary series at hand in case an investigation is rendered worthless by disturbance or ineptitude of any sort.

When we shall have undertaken simply those try-outs of a considerable number of single tests suggested above (cf. pp. 92 ff.), we shall certainly have enough at our command to arrange parallel series for each year: though there will be some difficulty in securing an approximate equivalence between the corresponding scales.

There has been some demand for yet another kind of extension of the scale. As it has appeared that the mental differences are extreme between one year and another in the case of the younger children, the need has been felt of *intermediate stages,* as for instance for specific standards for such age-levels as 6.5, 7.5 and 8.5 years. In our opinion this need is to be satisfied in another way, viz., by use of the mental quotient, since this permits us to take frac-

[28]Binet had five 9-year-old children tested twice with the same tests with a 14-day interval. On the average, the children passed 2.5 tests more on the second trial—an amount that would signify an increase of a half-year in mental age (pp. 164-5). As Bobertag has shown, the danger resident in repetition is not so great as this when the interval is longer (see above, p. 69); yet even under these conditions the use of the same tests is but a make-shift and a second and a third repetition of the same tests would be surely quite out of the question.

tions of ages into account without special half-year steps (see p. 105, below).

Finally, mention may be made of other desires, *curae posteriores:* differentiation of the scales for children of different social strata, for the two sexes, and especially series devoid of the speech factor for the testing of the deaf and dumb, etc.

(*d*) *The computation of the final values.* There are two main difficulties that demand our attention here.

The one consists in the limitation of the measures of the mental age and the chronological age to *whole numbers.* This necessity of using whole numbers must often entail an arbitrariness that renders impossible the carrying out of the method with precision.

For instance, a child who, when tested, lacks four months of completing his eighth year of life, must of necessity be classed as "8 years." If he passes the 7-year-old tests and two more, he still receives the mental age of 7 years, and is, accordingly, credited with a mental retardation of one year, although in reality there is practically no retardation at all.

Bobertag[29] tried to circumvent this difficulty by taking for his testing only those children that were close to their birthday (at least within 2 months). But usually there is no chance for free choice like this: there are certain children to be tested, regardless of what their age happens to be at the time. Besides, that kind of selection at most only lessens the difficulty for the chronological age, not for the mental age. The failure to consider the two or three excess tests passed still remains as a defect in the calculations.

---

[29] 40, I, p. 110.

Hence, however enticingly simple they may be, we shall have to give up the use of the rough whole-year designations, like 1, 2, 3 years of retardation, and make use of fractional values: it is enough, of course, to carry them to the first decimal place. In figuring mental age each single test passed in excess must, then, represent a fraction of a year. If, for example, two of the five 8-year tests are passed, then 2/5 is to be added to the mental age; the child in our example just above would then have obtained a mental age of 7.4 years. Terman and Childs (64) are already making use of such a mode of calculation, only theirs is made rather awkward by the presence of different fractional values in the several years: when the year contains seven tests, each test has only the value one-seventh, when five tests, one-fifth. This feature, too, confirms our desideratum already expressed that every one of the years should contain just five tests, then each test would have the same value, 0.2 of its year.

But now, once the use of the convenient whole numbers be given up, every objection against the introduction of the *mental quotient* is removed, for this furnishes us a single fractional value in place of the two fractional values, chronological age and mental age. This quotient lies for normal children in the neighborhood of 1.00 and grades off continuously from this value in both directions. As compared with the older method of dividing by the rough units of the age-levels, the use of the quotient has surely the advantage of affording a certain smoothness and continuity in the results, since the fraction (mental age divided by chronological age), when the decimals are used in each term, may assume any value whatever. Thus the mental quotient becomes not only a useful methodological device for the testing of abnormal children, but also a device to be recommended for use with normal individuals. We have already mentioned (p. 101) a case illustrative of its application.

The other difficulty of calculation pertains to the way in which scattered distribution of tests passed is handled in figuring mental age. As is well known, five scattered tests must be passed in order to add one year to the mental age, but no attention is then paid to the years in which these additional tests lie. Let us compare the two hypothetical examples which follow:

CHILD A.

All tests through the 6th year are passed: hence the basis for computation is a mental level of..................	6 years
also passed in Age 7 two tests also passed in Age 8 three tests also passed in Age 9 three tests also passed in Age 10 two tests	
total of 10 tests =	2 years
Resulting mental level..............................	8 years

CHILD B.

All tests through the 6th year are passed: hence the basis for computation is a mental level of..................	6 years
also passed in Age 7 three tests also passed in Age 8 five tests also passed in Age 9 two tests also passed in Age 10 no tests	
total of 10 tests =	2 years
Resulting mental level..............................	8 years

There seems no justification for equating these two children, because the first one really stands decidedly higher mentally by dint of his conspicuously good capacities in the higher levels. To be correct, we must credit more difficult tests (those lying in higher levels) with a larger fractional value than the tests normal to the age in question when we figure in these higher tests for addition to a lower age-level. We may propose a method of calculation for this purpose, that is not too complicated and that, like the mental quotient, takes account of the relation of the several years to each other. A test from a higher level used to supplement a failure in a lower level shall be counted not merely as one test, but as a quotient of the two years in question.

In our example just given, then, Child A would be figured out thus: basal point, mental age of 6 years; the tests from the four following years would be counted in this way:

Level 7 is formed by 2 tests from the 7th year (each of these counted therefore as "1 test") and by 3 tests from the 8th year, each of which are to be counted as 8/7 test). The 8th year would be formed by 3 tests from the 9th year (each counting 9/8 test) and 2 tests from the 10th year (each counting 10/8 test). We get, therefore, as total additional credits:

$$2 \times 1 = 2 \text{ tests}$$

$$3 \times \frac{8}{7} = 3.4 \text{ tests}$$

$$3 \times \frac{9}{8} = 3.4 \text{ tests}$$

$$2 \times \frac{10}{8} = 2.5 \text{ tests}$$

$$\overline{11.3 \text{ tests}}$$

Since every 5 tests are worth one mental year, the above value indicates a supplement of $11.3 \div 5 = 2.3$ mental years: so Child A gets a mental age of 8.3 years.

With Child B it works out thus: the 2 tests from age 9 serve to supplement age 7, and therefore have the value 9/7 each, the remaining 3 tests in the 7th year and likewise the 5 tests in the 8th year count for their own level, and thus figure 1 each.

$$3 \times 1 = 3 \text{ tests}$$

$$2 \times \frac{9}{7} = 2.6 \text{ tests}$$

$$5 \times 1 = 5 \text{ tests}$$

$$\overline{10.6 \text{ tests}}$$

These 10.6 tests indicate a supplement of 2.1 years; so Child, B gets a mental age of 8.1 years and his inferiority to Child A is now brought out statistically.

III. Estimation and Testing of Finer Gradations of Intelligence

(With the aid of the method of ranks)

1. *The Problem*

The different degrees of intelligence that are revealed by the Binet method are relatively gross: within any one of its age-levels there are possible other and very much finer gradations that escape detection by its tests. Yet these very differences are often enough just the ones of consequence, particularly whenever we are dealing with the members of a *relatively homogeneous group.* If, for instance, we are comparing the pupils of a school grade that are of approximately the same age and of corresponding school training, these pupils fall mostly into the same mental level according to the Binet-Simon tests, yet they occupy a finely graded scale of ranks within this level. Hence, the question *what place a pupil occupies among those of his age or of his class in respect to intelligence* must be answered by other methods that seek to establish a rank-order of the individuals concerned.

Rank-orders of the pupils of a class can be established in quite different ways. In the first place there is the *school* or pedagogical rank-order that is based on school performances. Thus we number the pupils according to the outcome of a school exercise:

the departmental teacher ranks them at the end of the term on the totality of their work in his subject: finally, all these ranks in different subjects are combined into a rank-order for the school certificate in which every pupil is assigned his "class-place."

Since these rank-orders are always available, it is but natural to employ them for our problem, and this is what actually happened very often in the early stages of the experimental study of intelligence. Thus, for example, Ebbinghaus (5) divided his subjects into three sections on the basis of their class-marks in order to determine whether the different groups responded with different degrees of success to his completion tests. Other investigators had the teachers select a number of 'good' and 'poor' scholars in order to make comparison of their behavior under experimentation.

Yet, however convenient this ever-ready classification may be, it is not at all adequate for our purposes, because the implicit assumption that underlies such uses of the class-marks—that school performance is an absolutely accurate indication of intelligence—is unjustified. The results obtained by the Binet-Simon method have already shown this (see p. 59), and other statistical data will confirm it. As a matter of fact, every school man who is blessed with psychological insight, knows it himself.

We need, then, a rank-order that is based directly upon the degree of intelligence of the pupils.

Such an order does not exist in the ordinary school system, and must therefore first be created *ad hoc*. There are available, again, two different ways of accomplishing this aim: either the teacher, on the basis of everything that he knows about his pupils, may *estimate* their intelligence and arrange them according to his estimate (see the next section) or we can apply *experimental tests* of intelligence, the outcome of which admits of arranging the pupils in a series. Rank-orders of intelligence are therefore divided into orders based on estimates and orders based on tests.

In the last resort the second of these divisions brings us to the question: *Is it possible, on the basis of a short examination with a series of tests to arrive at a gradation of pupils that corresponds with their actual differences of intelligence and such that the rank that each gains is sufficiently characteristic of his grade of intelligence within the group?*

It is not hard to obtain a rank-order on the basis of a test or of a series of tests. To be sure, the Binet tests, most of which admit of a choice between the evaluations 'right' or 'wrong,' are not fitted for that purpose, but we can obtain a gradation in all those tests that bring into operation a measurable performance, in which what is measured is the quantity of the performance in a given time or the quality of the performance (as indicated by the number of errors). Every test of this sort creates an array of ranks, only it remains to discover how much the obtained order may inform us about the intelligence of the examinees.

Hence we need here, too, a device for guaging our work, and this device consists in the comparison of several rank-orders obtained with the same individuals by means of the method of *correlation.*

The method of calculating correlation can not, of

course, be developed here.[1] We merely point out here that a correlation = 1.00 means that there is complete correspondence between the two rank-orders (or groups). A correlation = 0 means complete absence of correspondence. The size of the decimal fraction between 0 and 1, then, shows the degree of correspondence. The probable error (P. E.) is a measure of reliability: only when the correlation amounts to at least three times the size of its probable error is a real significance to be ascribed to it. In details the methods used by different investigators for calculating the coefficient of correlation show considerable differences. The appendix contains an example of the simplest method of calculating rank-correlation as I have used it.

All the different rank-orders that have been named can be brought into correlation with one another: of these possible correlations we shall have to deal for our purposes with: correlation of test with test, correlation of estimates with school performance, correlation of tests with estimates.

Correlations of tests with tests have been worked out in particular by Spearman (77, 79, 80). If the pupils of a class have been tested by means of several different tests and the resulting rank-orders show mutual high correlation, this is, in Spearman's opinion, a sign that the capacity operative in the tests depends upon a common factor (Spearman uses the expression "general intelligence" or "general ability"). This brings it about that Pupil A

[1]A general exposition of these methods will be found in Betz (70) and Stern (1, chs. 19 and 20). [Also in the translator's *Manual of Mental and Physical Tests*, Ch. 3.]

ranks high in the discrimination of line-lengths, in memory for nonsense syllables, etc., while Pupil Z ranks low in each of these functions. For, if the result were conditioned by specific abilities, a given pupil would occupy very different ranks in the different tests. Spearman has, indeed, found extraordinarily high correlations in some instances: on this account he holds it to be demonstrated that there really is such a thing as general intelligence, and that its grade can be experimentally determined by tests that correlate to a high degree with one another.

We can agree with the first of these conclusions. We have already alluded frequently in what has gone before to the 'general' and 'formal' character of intelligence, whose influence is operative in activities of widely differing character. Of course, we must admit that this influence of intelligence is never more than approximately uniform, that within the "general intelligence" of every person there exist certain specially strong and certain specially weak points, so that a truer picture of the total intelligence of the individual is given by the idea of a mutual balancing or compensation of different capacities than by the idea of their equality or correspondence.

But just here does the value of Spearman's method for the testing of intelligence become dubious. If we select four or five tests that show very high intercorrelations in order to use their totals as a measure of intelligence, there exists the danger that we may be testing by them only a very restricted portion of the field of intelligence and leaving entirely out of consideration other compensatorily important portions. If, on the other hand, we keep the idea of compensation in mind and therefore assemble together tests that correlate only moderately with one another, we have no way of knowing which combination of tests does actually secure that mutual balance on the basis of which as a whole a more correct quantitative expression of intelligence is to be yielded.

To the first of these points it can of course be replied: we can select tests that show a high correlation from such divergent realms of mental life that we shall avoid the danger of testing only a very restricted portion of the field of intelligence. But, in opposition to this, attention must be directed to a matter that has not been sufficiently heeded heretofore. All test investigations, even if they pertain to the most widely different realms of mental life, have this in common that they are experimental modes of procedure, so that all put the examinee into the same mental condition—that of being a subject. And this involves not only very definite adjustments of attention, of mood, etc., but also in particular the *habit of mere reacting,* of taking at a given moment a receptive attitude toward a problem set from without. Consequently, *spontaneous* intelligence is excluded by the conditions of the experiment; there is not involved that intelligence that sets its own problems, that thinks out things independently beyond what is immediately given, that anticipates explanations by questions, and that in the real situations of life quickly works out the best way of confronting a situation. And we have absolutely no way of knowing whether we can infer from the reactive intelligence, however many tests of it we make, to this spontaneous intelligence. It is possible that certain tests or certain combinations of tests have a fairly high correlation with the spontaneous intelligence, but that is something that can not be determined from the experiments.

Hence the mere comparison of tests with one another affords us neither a clear insight into the necessary compensations, nor a decision as to the symptomatic value of the testing; *rather must we seek the means of guaging the tests in some criterion that lies outside of experiment.* Such a criterion is supplied by the estimation of the pupils made by the teacher.

It follows that this estimation of intelligence by the teacher thus comes to possess a methodological significance of its own, for it can be set up as a standard for the comparison of other rank-orders, *i. e.*, those obtained experimentally, only when we have first made sure of its own nature and its reliability. There are two ways of going about this; the one is by analysis of the procedure of the teacher when he does the estimating of his pupils' intelligence, the other is by determining objectively to what extent his estimation is dependent upon what he knows about the pedagogical rank-order of the children, their places in the class or their examination marks, etc.

So, only when we have first discovered whether the estimated intelligence is a useful means of control or under what precautions it is useful, can the real experimental problem be attacked:—the problem of finding out those combinations of tests that correlate to a high degree and with great uniformity with a reliable set of estimations of intelligence. This matter will be the subject of the three sections that follow.

2. *The Teacher's Estimation of the Intelligence of his Pupils*

The question whether a teacher is really able to estimate the degree of intelligence of his pupils is one that has no little importance even outside of our special and limited problem. It is surely practically worth while for the teacher, who is accustomed ordinarily to pass judgments about his pupils primarily on the basis of their objective performance, to try for once to decide whether and to what extent a certain capacity, namely general intelligence, is concerned in these performances. He will be obliged to study his pupils more carefully, to analyze their individual disposition, and will perhaps come by this means to a better valuation of their work, to conclusions as to choice of curriculum, to advice as to the choice of vocations.

The estimation of intelligence has an advantage over the experimental testing of intelligence in the fact that it is based upon longer and wider acquaintance with the pupil. For months the teacher has watched the behavior of a pupil in the oral and written tasks of different studies, has noted his questions and answers, his interest or his indifference when dealing with many different subjects, his independence or his need of assistance in his work, and has seen as well his behavior when among his mates, in play in the school yard, on excursions, etc. He has, then, a much broader range of information on which to base his judgment of the pupil's intelligence than has the experimenter, who has merely taken a half-hour's time to record the response of the child to a small number of tests. But, on the other hand, there are some great disadvantages in this method. The teacher does not, as a rule, stop to consider on what concrete facts of observation his judgment is based: the symptoms which determine his judgment are not controllable as regards their real importance; when the intelligence of several pupils is compared, the comparison is based on different facts that are not strictly comparable with one another. Finally, the teacher is often by no means clear as to what he is to understand by 'intelligence' when he makes his decisions.

These considerations are enough to show that the estimation of intelligence is far from an easy matter, that it is not something to be demanded of every teacher as a matter of course. What is desired here is to seek the middle road between two opposite sources of danger: on the one hand we are threatened with the danger that the teacher can not free himself, when he estimates intelligence, from the pedagogical habit of judging his pupils by their schoolroom performance, in which event the rank-order for intelligence will be no more than a copy of the rank-order for class work, corrected in a few points. If the teacher tries to avoid this tendency, then there arises the other danger that he goes at the selection blindly and that the resulting rank-order becomes a mere product of chance.

Evidently, the estimating of intelligence by the teacher makes contribution not only to the psychology of the pupils, but also to the psychology of the teacher. Teachers will vary a great deal in their capacity to undertake this work of estimating intelligence, so that for scientific investigations it becomes methodologically essential that tests shall not be compared with any sort of estimation of intelligence made by any sort of teacher, but that *for this purpose teachers specially trained and specially gifted in psychology must be sought out and instructed specifically in the nature of the task demanded of them.*

An entertaining as well as instructive inquiry on this subject has been made by Binet (36; 71).

He sent to numerous elementary school teachers a questionary asking them to state: 1st, to what extent they thought that error might creep in when teachers sought to judge the intelligence of their pupils, and 2d, what method they would pursue in order to arrive at an accurate estimate of intelligence. Binet soon saw that he had thus found an excellent scheme for classifying the intelligence of the teachers.

The first question was not very well put. The answers simply showed that there were some optimists who thought that they practically never made any mistake in appraising the intelligence of their pupils, while others were ready to admit that they might be mistaken in one case in every three. Not much else came out of this question.

The answers to the second question were much more fruitful. The greatest variety of ideas concerning the nature of intelligence was exhibited: all possible attempts at defining it were made—all the way from the scholastic narrow-mindedness, which conceives intelligence as nothing but the capacity to acquire information, up to the neat formulation of one woman:

"L'intelligence ne sert pas seulement à apprendre, elle sert surtout à 'faire sa vie.'" And the symptoms on which the teachers base their judgment of intelligence! It is declared that heed must be given to heredity, since higher intelligence is to be expected from children of more intelligent parents. It is recommended to take note of the facial expression; the more intelligent child is easily distinguished from the mentally lazy, dull child by his vivacious, open, mobile countenance. Some of the teachers lay stress on observation of their pupils during periods of free play, and would regard as intelligent children that displayed initiative and creative tendencies there. But the chief insistence is laid, as would be expected, upon the behavior of the child under instruction, and the attempt is made, with more or less success, to differentiate the strictly intellectual factors in the school work from the phases that depend more on mere memory: quickness of apprehension, ability to solve problems in applied mathematics, understanding of historical movements and relations, good orthography, expressive reading and many other things are mentioned as symptoms that serve the teachers for estimating their pupils' intelligence. Finally, even the teachers themselves hit on the use of the method of tests by asking of their pupils certain questions, specially prepared for the purpose, the answers to which serve them as a measure for guaging intelligence.

Binet then enters into a very careful criticism of these various ideas, calls attention to the strong and the weak features in them, shows that the "intelligence questions" invented for the express purpose are much less useful than the tests worked out by the psychologist after long years of experimentation, and comes to the conclusion that the estimation of intelligence by the teacher is not at all likely to render the exact testing of intelligence a superfluous process. It must be admitted that he might easily have given more emphasis to the reverse of this statement: he might have pointed out that the estimation of intelligence may possess advantages that are excluded on principle from the mere test, so that the estimation may therefore be indispensable as a supplement, and also in part as a control for the results of tests.[2]

[2]This whole discussion of Binet's is couched in a light and sketchy vein, but is on that account one of the prettiest examples of the grace of his style and the pictorial clarity of his phrases. We may cite here just two instances that are so neatly put as to defy translation. Where he is speaking of the ease with which the possession of information may be misinterpreted as token of intelligence, he says: "La mémoire est la grande simulatrice de l'intelligence." And the recommendation to watch children while engaged in play as well as in school is coupled with the declaration: "En classe ils sont dénaturés par la discipline."

We shall bring together next the chief requirements that a teacher must keep in mind when he undertakes an estimation of intelligence if it is to be usable for scientific purposes.

He should conceive of intelligence, just as we defined it at the beginning of this monograph, as "general mental adaptability to new problems and conditions of life," should give particular heed to the two attributes "general" and "adaptation to the new," and should guard against identifying with intelligence any sort of special ability or the mere possession of information or readiness in speech. Because of the general nature of intelligence it is essential to take into consideration the way in which the child behaves in quite different situations and when confronted by problems of varied sorts.

But, now, it is of the essence of the estimation of intelligence that not only shall each pupil be judged individually, but he shall also be compared with the other pupils and be placed in a definite relation of equality or inequality with them. For this purpose of comparison there is to be laid down a rule that, despite its fundamental character, has by no means always been observed: *Only those pupils shold be located in a given rank-order of intelligence that are sufficiently like one another in other respects.* The reason is that the slight differences of intelligence that have to be considered in making the estimation have significance only when on the common basis of an otherwise homogeneous group. For this reason the comparative estimation of intelligence has usually been restricted to the pupils of a single class; but it is necessary as well to be careful to secure homogeneity within the class, not only by excluding children who are plainly abnormal, but also by limiting the estimation to a *definite range of ages.* If, for instance, in the 5th school year, normally corresponding to ages 10-11 years, the class contains some 13-year-old boys, they should not be included in a rank-order of intelligence, for the teacher is not in a position to determine what portion of the intelligence that they exhibit is to be ascribed to their greater age: that would have to be deducted even if they were compared to 11-year-old children. Hence, you must first sort out any class within which you would undertake an estimation of intelligence. It is impossible to lay down any hard and fast rule for this: the range of ages that should be included depends on different circumstances; a greater latitude of age is permissible in maturer than in the younger years. In general, the calculations that I shall speak of below indicate that some 20 to 25 per cent. of the members of every class must be excluded.

The arrangement of the pupils on the basis of their intelligence can be by groups or in a serial order. The first of these arrangements is far easier for the teacher. In fact, he is accustomed to classify almost all things that are judged in terms such that four to six classes are formed; and a similar schema can be applied to intelligence—as, for example, in the form: I very high intelligence, II good, III medium, IV slight, V very weak intelligence. Thus, Pearson and those of his followers who have made use of estimations of intelligence in their statistical investigations of school children have been content with groupings of this sort (74, 76, 81).

Personally, I do not find much to recommend in the method. Even though most of the pupils can be located without difficulty in one of the five groups, there still remains a fairly large number of pupils with whom the teacher remains in doubt as to which of two adjacent groups they may belong to. The final decision is then an arbitrary one, which, if often enough repeated, can destroy the value of the whole distribution. If, for instance, three such doubtful cases are assigned to Group II the proportioning of cases and the resulting correlations are quite different from what they would be if these cases had been assigned to Group III, where they might just as properly be placed. It follows that so small a number of groups as this is entirely inadequate for the most important problems of correlation. Many of our tests yield finely graded rank-orders of pupils, and so it is to be desired that the estimated intelligence with which these tests are to be related should also take the form of a rank-order.

The construction of a rank-order of all pupils based on estimations of their intelligence in this way naturally presents many difficulties. Many persons hold it as a matter of course to be quite impossible. But experience has shown that the task can be done. The division into groups that we have just discussed can, indeed, be carried out as a preliminary step; then the pupils within each of the groups must be further arranged in a scale, so far as practicable. At the limits of the groups, however, care must be taken, for it has been shown many times that shifts will have to be made at these points, as, for instance, a child originally assigned to Group II has to be placed after the children lying in the upper section of Group III.

But, on the other hand, the principle of rank-arrangement must not be carried so far as to insist on assigning a precise place to every child at any cost. Often enough, especially in the middle region, it will be felt to be an arbitrary matter to give *N* a poorer place than *M*, because it will have been impossible to arrive at an unequivocal judgment as to the difference in the worth of the intelligence displayed by the two children. The rule for such cases is to give the same rank-number to individuals of equivalent ability, using the number that corresponds to the average of the places that they occupy. Thus, if four individuals that would have occupied the stations 5, 6, 7 and 8 seem of equal intelligence, each one receives the rank-number 6.5, *i. e.*, $\frac{5+6+7+8}{4} = 6.5$.

In case this process has to be followed repeatedly, the number of rank-differences that are at our disposal is reduced, but this disadvantage is more than compensated for by the advantage of avoiding arbitrariness in the arrangement. It is no misfortune if no more than 20 or even a dozen different rank-numbers are forthcoming in the ranking of a class of 30 pupils.

We shall be obliged to dwell somewhat longer on the matter, already broached, of the dependence of the series of estimations on the pedagogical rank-order. The greater the rôle played by the school's rank-order in the ordinary management of the class, the greater will be this dependence. But there prevail decided differences with regard to the class-marks. The plan, which was formerly quite generally followed, whereby each pupil had a "class-place," which determined his rank among his class-mates for a quarter of a year, is now becoming less and less common. Sometimes the statement of standing is accompanied by a designation of place in the class, *e. g.*, "promoted as 15th in a class of 27," without laying any further special stress on the ranking; sometimes even this designation is lacking, so that there exists no positive school rank-order at all. Of course, even where there is a school rank-order, it is to be desired that the teacher work out his estimation of intelligence as far as possible independently of this school ranking. On this account it is in every way objectionable to proceed, as is often done because it is the easiest way, by taking the school ranking as a starting point and simply shifting the position of those children whose rank in this list has been displaced by some special circumstance, like illness, transfer of school, evident laziness, etc. Burt, for example, worked in that way. To be sure, such a "corrected school ranking" is doubtless better than an uncorrected one for psychological purposes, but it by no means presents a correct ranking of intelligence.

To secure as impartial a ranking of intelligence as possible, the following procedure may be recommended. Write the names of each of the pupils to be ranked on a separate card, and arrange these first in alphabetical order. Then and only then sort out the cards into different groups for their intelligence, and finally try to settle upon rankings within each group. The series thus secured is then noted down with the proper number for each individual.

It is an excellent plan to do the work all over again after an interval of perhaps three or four weeks, and without referring to the series first obtained. The degree of correspondence between the two estimations is then to be determined by the correlation method. Only if the coefficient of reliability is high, *i. e.*, if the two series are very similar to one another, should they be made the basis of further investigations. If they are then to be used, it is best to construct an amalgamated series out of the two estimations by taking for each pupil the mean of the two rank-numbers that he has obtained and bringing together these means for the new rank-order.

Distinct differences in method will appear when the estimation of intelligence is made in elementary schools (*Volksschule*) than when in higher schools.

The elementary school teacher has the particular advantage that he is usually the only teacher of the class, and thus can observe the behavior of the children in the most varied activities, in technical and theoretical subjects, at play and at work. But just this very breadth of information also renders him in a certain sense less independent in his estimation. Because his knowledge of his pupils extends in so comprehensive a manner over their school performances; all their grades and the determination of their class-places are the product of a single teacher, so that it is psychologically easily intelligible that he can not so easily free himself from this judgment that he has himself worked out, even when he undertakes the entirely different problem of estimating their intelligence.

With the teacher in the higher schools the situation is different. He instructs only in certain subjects and thus comes to know his pupils only partially. This certainly renders the estimation of their intelligence difficult. The departmental teacher must especially guard against identifying special talent or lack of talent in his special subject with general intelligence or the lack of it. Yet he is less biassed in his construction of a rank-order by the same circumstances, in that the rank-order of the school, if there be one, is never his own work that might affect his judgment by auto-suggestion, but is something that has been obtained by the mere mechanical addition of all the different performances of the pupils, including performances in other subjects with which he has nothing to do. And this entails a further advantage, viz., that estimations of the intelligence of the same group of pupils can be obtained from the different departmental teachers who instruct them, and that these estimations can then be compared with each other and finally amalgamated into a single series. Of course, for the purpose of making a comparison of this sort only those teachers should be drawn upon whose subjects of instruction can afford a basis for a fairly exact knowledge of the pupils—not, then, some teacher who might give instruction to the class in some minor accessory subject only.

It is evident, also, that teachers can be asked to make estimations of their pupils' intelligence only after they have become intimate with them—not, for instance, right after the beginning of the school year. Teachers that have accompanied a class and known them more than a single year supply especially favorable conditions for the work.

3. *Estimated Intelligence and School Performance*

These theoretical considerations may now be illustrated by a series of quantitative results that bear on the relation between estimated intelligence and school performance. I shall make use of some already published material of English origin and also of some as yet unpublished material that has been gathered as opportunity offered by members of the psychological department at Breslau.

In the English investigations (Table XV) the school performance has been measured in different ways; in some there were used the class-places, in others the results of school examinations, which are held regularly in all classes in England. Unfortunately, the special methodological measures that were taken in securing the estimated intelligence are not precisely enough reported to permit us to pass any judgment concerning the reliability of the results.

In all cases there are clear, and in some high correlations—decidedly higher, it is to be noted, between intelligence and the results of examinations than between intelligence and class-place (0.76 as compared with 0.68). This result is not without interest. So far as we may judge from the account of the investigation, the estimation of intelligence had been undertaken without the results of the examinations having been known—indeed, in some

TABLE XV

Investigator	Burt (72)	Burt (72)	Jones (76)	Gilby and Pearson (74)
Type of school	Elementary	Higher	Elementary	Elementary
Number of pupils	30	13	249	1725
Ages of pupils	12.5—13.5	12.5—13.5	Corrected for same age and same class	
Kind of estimate	Rank-order	Rank-order	Four groups	Five Groups
Correlation with school rank-order	....	....	....	0.67
Correlation with school examination	0.81	0.78	0.70	0.68
Correlation with other estimates of the same pupils	0.88	0.91	....	....

Investigator	Waite (81)	Waite (81)	Average of all values
Type of school	Higher	Higher	
Number of pupils	182	238	
Ages of pupils	Corrected for same age and same class		
Kind of estimate	Five groups	Five groups	
Correlation with school rank-order	0.74	0.63	0.68
Correlation with school examination	0.82	....	0.76
Correlation with other estimates of the same pupils	....	....	0.89

cases before these had taken place. The estimates, then, were not affected by the ranking in the school tests, and the rather high correlation could therefore be regarded as a reliable expression of the degree of correspondence between intelligence and the work done in the examinations. Burt also had estimates of intelligence of the same pupils made by different teachers and by disinterested school-mates of the pupils. The correlations between these estimates are very high, but since all those who estimated set out from the already known rank-order of the pupils, which they had merely to correct, it follows that this high correspondence is nothing remarkable and that it has no scientific value.

In the course of discussions of this subject in the meetings of the Psychological Seminary at Breslau, during the winter semester 1911-12, the need became evident of clearing up the methodological aspects of the whole subject of estimating intelligence by trials of our own. Fortunately, two of our members, who were engaged in practical school work, were ready to secure new material.[3] The results thus obtained are worth noting because they very clearly demonstrate the methodological difficulties and the way to overcome them and also bring out the necessary difference between the procedure in secondary and in elementary schools.

Principal Rindfleisch had the teachers in charge of a boys' *Volksschule* prepare for their classes lists that showed both the ranking of the pupils on the

[3]Hearty thanks are due to Principal Rindfleisch (Liegnitz) and Dr. Scheifler (a high-school teacher at Görlitz) for their great pains and for their courtesy in placing the material at my disposal.

basis of their performances and also their ranking according to their intelligence. So far as it has proved feasible I have calculated the rank-correlations of these lists. It must be stated that quite a number of the lists had to be excluded; some because the teacher had been satisfied to present the material arranged in a very few intelligence-groups, and some because the necessary precautions of method had plainly not been observed. Thus, there were many lists that showed plainly that the rank-order for school performances had been arranged first and then the rank-order for intelligence had been arranged from it with only a very few corrections.

TABLE XVI

VOLKSCHULE LIEGNITZ

Class	School Year	Age	Number Tested	Number Omitted	ϱ	P. E.
VIa	1.	6.3-7.6	47	8	0.85	± 0.05
VIb	1.	6.0-7.1	37	16	0.78	± 0.07
Vb	2.	7.7-8.7	40	7	0.47	± 0.1
			(34)	(13	(0.74	± 0.08)
IVa	3.	8.3-10.0	45	13	0.87	± 0.05
IIIa	4.	9.3-11.6	43	11	0.88	± 0.05
IIa	5.	10.3-12.2	30	14	0.97	± 0.03
Ia	6.	11.6-13.6	30	12	0.91	± 0.05

The remaining lists, however, cover all the different school grades. The important data are shown in Table XVI. There it will be noted that in figuring the correlation I left out in each class a number of pupils whose age exceeded the proper limits. If we leave Class Vb out of consideration for the moment, the correlations are then uniformly markedly high—between .78 and .97; average without Class Vb = 0.88. The fact that the correlation is higher than the

English correlation between estimated intelligence and class-place is doubtless due to the circumstance that the English were content to use a small number of classificatory groups of intelligence, whereas in our lists serial ranking was required. This more difficult task brought out a somewhat higher dependence on the school ranking, which was known by the teachers and in fact prepared by them. Hence this very high correlation is not a proper expression of the actual degrée of connection between intelligence and school work, as will be seen more clearly upon a closer analysis of the lists. There are certain symptoms by which one can tell very positively whether the teacher has or has not made the attempt to free himself from the suggestive influence of the school ranking; and the more seriously this attempt was made, the smaller was the correlation.

Mention must be made in this connection of the Class Vb, whose teacher plainly undertook the work with great independence and with fine psychological comprehension. This teacher settled the numbering for his intelligence series without glancing at his school-work series and sought to explain the cases of special discrepancy between school performance and intelligence by brief remarks ("moved in from the country," "sick a long time," "poor home conditions," etc.). The result was astonishing—a correlation of only 0.47.

This one correlation is, in my opinion, psychologically and methodologically more important than the much higher ones obtained for the other classes, because the lack of higher correlation is certainly due not to any peculiar composition of the Class Vb, but to the special care and capacity for judging of the teacher who did the estimating.

I have made a further calculation for this Class Vb by excluding those six pupils in whose cases there existed, according to the teacher's notes, special conditions. The correlation for the remaining 34 then rose at once to 0.74; in other words, it approximated very closely the lowest correlations computed for the other classes. From this it follows for this particular class, and presumably as a general principle, too, that the low correlation first secured is not due to any distinct thorough-going discrepancy between degree of intelligence and school efficiency, but rather to an unusual discrepancy between endowment and performance in a minority of the pupils. This small group demands the special consideration of the teacher and individual treatment, for it is with them that the danger is greatest that the ordinary valuation of the children in terms of their school work may lead to an erroneous appraisement and handling.

Turning to the *higher schools,* I have at my disposal now a single class only, but the estimation of the intelligence of this class has special value on account of the great thoroughnrss and precautions of method adopted, and on account of the have that several teachers joined in estimating the same children. Table XVII exhibits the correlations that I have computed. I have to thank thhavgular master of the class for the material.

The class was an *Untertertia* grade in a *Gymnasium.*[4] The regular teacher (Teacher A) was well

[4]This would correspond scholastically approximately to our first high-school year.—*Translator.*

trained psychologically and as a member of my seminary understood perfectly the things to be kept in mind in estimating intelligence. As he had already taught these pupils the year before and had given them during the current year ten hours of instruction a week (Latin and French), it may be taken for granted that he possessed a really exact acquaintance with the material before him. It can therefore be said that his estimation of their intelligence was made under specially favorable conditions. Moreover, he had two other teachers estimate the same pupils. Of these, Teacher, it is true, instructed the class only two hours a week in history and Teacher C four hours a week in religion and German. The instructions were to judge the children not on the basis of the particular ability that they might have displayed in the subjects the teachers taught, but on the basis of the impression of their general intelligence. Beside these three estimated orders there was also available the series of 'class-places' of the pupils. In making my calculations I excluded eight pupils who were too old. There remained 23—enough to permit the reckoning of valid correlations. Now a first glance at the table shows that the correlation between intelligence and class-place is much lower than those obtained in most of the elementary school classes. The specially reliable estimation of Teacher A gives a correlation of 0.43. Of those for the two other teachers, the one is somewhat higher, the other somewhat lower. When we combine the estimates of all three teachers into an amalgamated estimation-series, we obtain again a correlation with the class-place of 0.45—a value that coincides almost exactly with that of the single elementary class Vb that we have accorded special treatment. *Hence it appears that when an estimation of intelligence is made with special thoroughness and caution, there exists only a moderate degree of correlation between it and school efficiency.*

TABLE XVII

Class: U III of a Gymnasium (7th school year).
Ages of those investigated: 13.5 to 14.5 years.
Number investigated: 23 (8 others omitted as too old).
Number of teachers estimating: 3 (Teacher A the principal teacher).

Correlations between estimated intelligence and class-place:	
Teacher A and Class-Place	0.43 ± 0.13
Teacher B and Class-Place	0.55 ± 0.12
Teacher C and Class-Place	0.33 ± 0.14
Teachers B and C (combined) and Class-Place	0.49 ± 0.13
Teachers A, B and C (combined) and Class-Place	0.45 ± 0.13
Intercorrelations of the Estimations:	
Teacher B and Teacher A	0.69 ± 0.10
Teacher C and Teacher A	0.65 ± 0.12
Teachers B and C (combined) and Teacher A	0.75 ± 0.10

The values obtained for all three of the secondary school teachers alike show that it is much easier for the individual teacher in the secondary school to rid himself from the influence of the class arrangement, because this arrangement has not been determined by himself alone.

The reliability of the result is augmented by the *intercorrelation* of the series of the teachers. These correlations are, in fact, much higher: highest (0.75) when the estimates of the two supplementary teachers are combined and related to the particularly trustworthy estimate of the regular class-teacher. That is to say, then, the estimation of intelligence undertaken by the teachers quite independently of one another exhibit a great similarity to one another, despite the fact that the several teachers derived their judgments from observations in quite different school subjects. *This decided correspondence of the judgments of the teachers on their pupils' intelligence, taken in conjunction with the fair degree of independence of their judgment from the class-place, seems to me to be a forcible argument for the scientific usefulness of the method of intelligence estimation.* But the result also teaches us, when we compare with it the experience gained in the elementary school, that only such estimations of intelligence are useful as have been carried out by an exact method and with special psychological knowledge.

4. *Rank-orders of Intelligence obtained by Tests*

We can now return once more to the starting point of this whole section, the experimental testing of intelligence. For we may safely regard the estimation of intelligence by the teachers, when undertaken with the necessary precautions, as a suitable control-device by which we can measure the reliability of experimental testing.

The material just now available on the correlation between rank-orders obtained by tests and those obtained by estimations is, to be sure, very scanty, yet it is already enough to indicate the direction in which greater results are to be looked for. Here, too, do we come upon that principle that we found universally applicable in intelligence testing: no single test of whatever kind, but only a *skillfully combined system of tests* yields a reliable gradation of intelligence.

Burt in England and Ries in Germany have carried on with normal children investigations pertaining to this field. Burt deals with but a small number of cases:—one group of 30 'elementary' school-pupils and another of 13 'secondary' pupils; Ries has investigated five classes in an elementary school. The very much more extensive and precise investigations of the Breslau teacher, Hylla, have unfortunately not yet been completed.

Burt (72) tested his classes with 12 different tests. The rank-orders obtained for the different tests show quite different correlations with the estimated rank-order—six tests over 0.50, six tests under 0.50. The tests that show the higher correlations are mostly those that pertain to attention, motor skill and memory. These tests and their correlations are shown in Table XVIII. On the other hand, the tests of discriminative sensitivity uniformly show very low correlations with intelligence—a result worthy of note because there still prevails a tendency in many quarters to use sensory tests for testing intelligence.

TABLE XVIII

BURT'S EXPERIMENTS WITH NORMAL CHILDREN

Test	Correlation with Est. Intell.	
	Elem. School	Secndry School
1. Dotting. (A zig-zag row of dots traveling at constant speed must be hit with a pencil)	0.60	0.84
2. Spot pattern. (A group of dots to be reproduced by drawing after 5 exposures in a tachistoscope)	0.76	0.75
3. Mirror. (A pattern visible only in a mirror is to be pierced at marked points)	0.67	0.54
4. Memory span for concrete and abstract words and nonsense syllables	0.57	0.78
5. Alphabet. (Cards with the letters of the alphabet are to be properly arranged)	0.61	0.80
6. Sorting (50 playing cards of 5 different colors are to be sorted into 5 packs)	0.52	0.56
Resulting rank-order for all 6 tests	0.85	0.91

The correlations found by Burt are in general somewhat lower for the elementary than for the higher school, but no particular value is to be ascribed to the higher correlations on account of the small number, 13, of subjects in the second group.

Ries[6] used two methods: Method A is patterned after the Ranschburg method of word-pairs; each word-pair is comprised of two words that stand in a causal relation to one another, *e. g.*, 'hunger'—'weakness.' Each pair was pronounced and their retention tested by the method of right associates. Method B was in the form of an association experiment: to each word pronounced there was to be given as a response a word whose meaning stood in the relation of effect to cause with the stimulus word. In both methods the plan was to bring intelligence into action by the use of logical relations. And in fact the results did furnish a very high correlation with estimated intelligence and with a small probable error, viz.: with Method A 0.59, 0.85, 0.89, 0.86 and 0.90 (in the different classes) and with Method B 0.85, 0.94, 0.86, 0.91.

A supplementary test undertaken for comparative purposes by means of the Ebbinghaus completion method gave in two classes somewhat smaller correlations.

Ries' results doubtless show that the methods that he proposes may lay claim to a place in a system of tests for securing rank-orders of intelligence. On the other hand, it should not be concluded from the

---

[6]Reference 78. See also the extensive critical review of Ries by Bobertag, *Zeits. f. angew. Psych.*, 5, p. 207.

high correlations that Method A or Method B taken alone are adequate for testing and ranking intelligence. For, in the first place, Ries' results do not

TABLE XIX

Ries' experiments on 24 boys (*Mittelschule*, 2d class, ages 12-14).
Test A: Method of word-pairs and right associates.
Test B: Association of effect to a given cause.

Correlation of Test A with Test B	0.61
Correlation of Test A with Estimated Intelligence	0.85
Correlation of Test B with Estimated Intelligence	0.94
Correlation of Tests A and B (combined) with Est. Int.	0.98

present the requisite uniformity (in one class, Method A correlated with estimated intelligence by only 0.59), and it is very questionable whether repetition of the tests in other places would furnish the same high correlations. Again, each of his methods tests only one phase of intelligence, and a comparison of the two methods with one another shows how little right we have to infer one phase from the other. Thus, Ries gives for one class a table of the original data from which I have been able to calculate some results not mentioned by him (Table XIX). The result is that the two methods do not correlate at all highly with one another, only 0.61; in other words, the ranking of intelligence by Method A furnishes a distribution of stations that is in some parts quite different from the distribution furnished by Method B.

The example is, however, excellently adapted to point out the way toward the method that is to be applied.

What does it mean that both tests correlate so high with estimated intelligence, but so low with one another? Plainly, this is possible only when the rank-orders obtained by the tests deviate from the rank-order obtained by estimation *in contrary directions* in some portions of the series.

In illustration: if a pupil obtains Station 10 in the estimated rank-order, Station 8 in the order of Test A and Station 12 in the order of Test B, and if a similar thing occurs with other pupils, then the above-mentioned differences in the correlations follow of necessity. But it is equally evident that the combining of the two stations for tests, 8 and 12, gives the so-called "resulting rank-place for tests," 10, a value that now coincides with the station for estimated rank-order. The two tests therefore mutually compensate one another and thus form, when combined, a measure of intelligence that comes much nearer the estimated intelligence than either test by itself. Put psychologically, the tests demand the activity of aspects of intelligence so different as to be very unequally developed in one and the same person, but which, taken together, do characterize his degree of intelligence.

And, as a matter of fact, the correlation computed from Ries' data did figure out so that the amalgamated rank-order for the two tests presents the extraordinarily high correlation with estimated intelligence of 0.98.

In this way, then, the mutual compensation of tests that we have already set forth as a requirement, becomes a controlling principle of the test-series, and the correlation method gives us a numerical device for discovering that combination of tests in which we approach most nearly to perfect compensation. I mean that we must combine together tests that correlate less with one another than each one of them correlates with estimated intelligence, and that combination whose amalgamated rank-order shows the highest and most constant correlation with estimated intelligence is the system of tests that we seek. Naturally, we shall not limit ourselves to two tests in making our system, but shall combine a larger number into one compensation-system.

This was the idea that incited Hylla to the investigations previously mentioned which are still in progress. The idea of compensation as a principle in assembling tests has already arisen simultaneously both in England and in France.

Thus, from the tests that had afforded the highest correlations with estimated intelligence in his investigations, Burt worked out an amalgamated rank-order whose correlation with estimated intelligence considerably exceeded all the single correlations (Table XVIII). In the elementary school the single correlations ranged between 0.52 and 0.76, that of their combination amounted to 0.85; in the higher schools the single correlations ranged between 0.54 and 0.84, while the correlation for the combined tests rose to 0.91. From this Burt draws the conclusion (pp. 158-9): "By means, then, of some half-dozen tests, we are able independently to arrange a group of boys in an order of intelligence, which shall be decidedly more accurate than the order given by scholastic examination, and probably more accurate than the order given by the master, based on personal intercourse during two or three years, and formulated with unusual labor, conscientiousness and care."

This conclusion sounds extremely optimistic indeed, since the material that Burt had at his disposal, 43 subjects, does not in the slightest degree suffice for the formulation of such a thesis. However, the principle that it embodies is so promising and so illuminating as imperatively to demand a thorough retesting by the most exact methods and on a very extensive scale.

An analogous result has been found also with *feeble-minded* children. Mlle. Descoeudres (73) tested 14 children in an institution by means of 15 different tests. It is true that the children differed very greatly in age (from 6.5 to 14 years), yet it was possible to estimate their intelligence by the general impression that they made in the house and in the

TABLE XX

DESCOEUDRES: EXPERIMENTS ON FEEBLE-MINDED CHILDREN

Tests	Correlat'ns with Est. Intell.: of each test	of each 5 tests	of all the tests combined
1. Comparison of terms	0.878		
2. Computation	0.868		
3. Describing pictures	0.842	0.91	
4. Problem-questions	0.817		
5. Tactual discrimination	0.812		
6. Definitions	0.801		
7. Stringing beads	0.780		
8. Inventiveness (a picture is shown: what are the persons in it talking about?)	0.761	0.84	0.99
9. 'Patience' (restoring a cut-up picture)	0.734		
10. Knowing four coins	0.699		
11. Attention (cancelling *a*'s)	0.671		
12. Visual memory (5 objects)	0.646		
13. Noting omissions in drawings	0.637	0.73	
14. Auditory memory (5 words)	0.539		
15. Naming 60 words in 3 min	0.509		

schoolroom and to arrange them in order on this basis. The first column of figures in Table XX shows the correlations of the several tests with the estimated rank-order. The correlations are arranged in order of their magnitude and run from 0.88 to 0.51. Mlle. Descoeudres also calculated the amalgamated rank-order for all the tests and found a correlation of 0.99 between it and estimated intelligence—almost complete correspondence, then, between the two series. I have not myself checked up this value to see if it is absolutely correct, but I have from the original data calculated the correlation with intelligence for each 5 tests, taken in combination (Column 2) and in each case I found confirmation of the rule that the amalgamated correlation was considerably higher than the highest correlation of any single one of the tests of which it was compounded.

A few hints may be added concerning certain other points to be observed in working at the problem of ranking by tests.

(*a*) *Measurability.* It must be possible to express the performance in the test conveniently and unequivocally by a numerical value: and these numerical values must make sufficient differentiation within a group that a rank-order of performance can be drawn up.

(*b*) *Reliability.* A test is reliable only when its outcome is a true expression of abilities and is not too much affected by variable and temporary conditions. Reliability is tested by applying the same (or an analogous) test several times to the same group of subjects. Only if these repeated testings show a high degree of intercorrelation is the test valid scientifically.

(*c*) *Fairly high correlation*, even of the single test, *with estimated intelligence.* Because tests that of themselves exhibit little or no relation to intelligence can not, of course, gain symptomatic significance for intelligence by combination, however many of them are combined.

(*d*) *Comprehensiveness* of the tests, and that in two directions. First, we should endeavor to bring into action the different functions concerned in intelligence (see above, pp. 20 f.). Secondly, we should take care that the numerical records refer not only to quantity, but also to the quality of the performance, *e. g.*, both to the number of units accomplished in a given time and also to the percentage of errors made during the work.

(*e*) We should see to it that the *estimation of intelligence* be done thoroughly and conscientiously.

(*f*) When a considerable number of tests have been carried out upon a group, then combine the results into different amalgamated rank-orders until that combination has been found that yields the strongest correlation with the estimated intelligence. The combination should then be tested out on other groups.

The construction of an amalgamated rank-order is very easy. The ranks obtained by each subject in the several tests are combined into an average value. These average values themselves do not form the series desired, but must first be revised into ordinal numbers that represent the final rank-order.

Example: The pupils have been tested in three tests. The best pupil has obtained in the three trials the rank-places 3, 1, 1, the second-best the places 1, 2, 4, the third the places 2, 4, 2, etc. The averages are for Pupil A $\frac{3+1+1}{3} = 1.67$, for B $\frac{1+2+4}{3} = 2.33$, for C $\frac{2+4+2}{3} = 2.67$. Hence, in the final or amalgamated series, A receives the Rank-place 1, B Place 2, C Place 3.

If we proceed in this manner we may, I think, expect that the method of amalgamated ranks can be worked out into a systematized plan of procedure, as has already been done with the method of age-levels.

Not until we combine both these ideas can we hope to master the whole field of intelligence testing. The system of levels draws the great wave-lines of mental development: the method of ranking sketches the finer ripples within each level, and in such a manner that the precise evaluation of the degree of intelligence of the individual child shall be possible. At the same time, the purely psychological analysis of the behavior of the subject toward the test must not be neglected, because it supplements the quantitative determination of intelligence by making it possible to ascertain the qualitative 'coloring' of the intelligence in the individual case.

BIBLIOGRAPHY

BIBLIOGRAPHY.

The following abbreviations are used:

AmJPs = American Journal of Psychology.
AnPs = L'Année psychologique.
ArdePs = Archives de psychologie.
BrJPs = British Journal of Psychology.
EPd = Die experimentelle Pädagogik.
JEdPs = Journal of Educational Psychology.
JNeMeDis = Journal of Nervous and Mental Diseases.
JPsAsth = Journal of Psycho-Asthenics.
PdSe = Pedagogical Seminary.
PsCl = Psychological Clinic.
PsMon = Psychological Monographs (Review Pub. Co.).
TrSc = The Training School.
ZAngPs = Zeitschrift für angewandte Psychologie.
ZEPd = Zeitschrift für experimentelle Pädagogik.
ZNPt = Zeitschrift für die gesamte Neurologie und Psychiatrie.
ZPdPs = Zeitschrift für pädagogische Psychologie.
ZPs = Zeitschrift für Psychologie.

A fairly complete bibliography of intelligence testing up to the summer of 1911 will be found in

1. W. Stern. Die differentielle Psychologie in ihren methodischen Grundlagen. Leipzig, 1911.

On this account we give in the bibliography that follows only the together with all the publications that are not contained in the earlier list (designated by an asterisk). The starred references, then, save for a few additions, represent the rich productivity of the last year (summer of 1911 to September of 1912).

A. On the Introduction and Part I.

(Single Tests and Series of Tests.)

See also literature cited in Reference 1, pp. 426-431.

2. A. Binet. Attention et adaptation. *AnPs*, 6: 1900, 248-404.

*3. A. Binet. A propos de la mesure de l'intelligence. *AnPs*, 11: 1905, 69-82.

4. M. Dosai-Révész. Exp. Beitrag z. Psychol. der moralisch verkommenen Kinder. *ZAngPs*, 5: 1911, 272-330.

5. H. Ebbinghaus. Ueber eine neue Methode zur Prüfung geistiger Fähigkeiten u. ihre Anwendung bei Schulkindern. *ZPs*, 13: 1897, 401-459.

*6. S. I. Franz. Handbook of mental examination methods. *JNeMeDisMon* No. 10, 1912. Pp. 165.

*7. W. Healy and G. M. Fernald. Tests for practical mental classification. *PsMon*, 1911. No. 54. Pp. 53.

8. K. Heilbronner. Zur klinisch-ps. Untersuchungstechnik. *Monatsschrift f. Psychiatrie*, 17: 1905, 117-132.

*9. E. B. Huey. Backward and feeble-minded children. *EdPsMon*, 1912.

*10. E. B. Huey. Retardation and the mental examination of retarded children. *JPsAsth*, 15: 1910, 31-43.

11. Intelligenzproblem und Schule. Bericht über den zweiten Verhandlungstag des I. Kongresses f. Jugendbildung u. Jugendkunde zu Dresden, Oct., 1911. *Arbeiten des Bundes f. Schulreform*, 5: 1911.

12. K. Jaspers. Die Methoden der Intelligenzprüfung und der Begriff der Demenz. Krit. Referat. *ZNPt*, Ref. 1, 1910, 401-452.

*12a. R. H. Johnson and J. Gregg. Three new psychometric tests. *PdSe*, 19: 1912, 201-203.

*12b. Kurtze. Intelligenzprüfung. *Zeits. f. Beh. Schwachsinn.*, 32: 1912, 69-79.

*13. O. Lipmann. Katalog der Ausstellung des Inst. f. ang. Ps. u. ps. Sammelforschung. Bericht über den V. Kong. f. exp. Ps. in Berlin. 1912.

14. E. Meumann. Intelligenzprüfung an Kindern der Volksschule. *EPd*, 1: 1905, 35-100.

15. E. Meumann. Der gegenwärtige Stand der Methodik der Intelligenzprüfung. *ZEPd*, 11: 1910, 68-79.

*16. E. Meumann. Ueber eine neue Methode der Intelligenzprüfung und über den Wert der Kombinationsmethoden. *ZPdPS*, 13: 1912, 145-163.

*17. Meyer. Die Bedeutung der modernen Psychologie f. d. Militärwesen. *Neue Militär. Blätter*. 1911, 53 Jahrg., Nos. 6, 9, 10.

*18. Meyer. Psychologie und militärische Ausbildung. *ZPdPs*, 13 (2), 81-85.

19. H. Münsterberg. Finding a life work. *McClure's Mag.*, 1910, 398-403.

*20. H. Münsterberg. Experimentalpsychologie und Berufswahl. *ZPdPs*, 13: 1912, 1-7.

*21. C. S. Myers. The pitfalls of 'mental tests.' *Brit. Med. Jour.*, 28, I, 1911. (Also in German by Bobertag, *ZAngPs*, 6 (1), 60-65.)

22. E. Rodenwalt. Aufnahmen des geistigen Inventars Gesunder als Massstab für Defektprüfungen bei Kranken. *Monatsschrift f. Psychiatrie*, 17: Ergänzungsheft, 1905, 17-84.

23. G. Rossolimo. Allgemeine Characteristik der ps. Profile, 1. Geistig-minderwertige Kinder, 2. Nerven- und Geisteskranke. Moscow, 1910. Pp. 106.

24. G. Rossolimo. Psychologische Profile. Die Methodik. Moscow, 1910. Pp. 52.

*24a. G. Rossolimo. Die ps. Profile. Zur Methodik der quantitativen Untersuchung der psychischen Vorgänge in normalen und pathol. Fällen. *Klinik f. ps. Krankheiten*, 6: 1911 (3), 46; (4), 32.

25. S. de Sanctis. Typen und Grade mangelhafter geistiger Entwicklung. *Eos*, 2: 1905, 97-115.

*26. R. Sommer. Ueber die Methoden der Intelligenzprüfung. *Klinik f. psychol. u. nerv. Krankh.*, 7: 1912, 1-21.

27. J. van der Torren. Ueber das Auffassungs- und Unterscheidungsvermögen f. optische Bilder bei Kindern. *ZAngPs*, 1: 1908, 189-232.

28. G. M. Whipple. Manual of mental and physical tests. Baltimore, 1910. 2d ed., 1914.

*29. Mary T. Whitley. An empirical study of certain tests for individual differences. *Archives of Psychol.*, 19. New York, 1911. Pp. 146.

30. T. Ziehen. Die Prinzipien und Methoden der Intelligenzprüfung. Berlin, 1908. 3d ed., 1911. Pp. 94.

B. On Part II.

(Binet-Simon Method.)

See also literature cited in Reference 1, pp. 431-432.

*31. L. P. Ayres. The Binet-Simon measuring scale for intelligence. Some criticisms and suggestions. *PsCl*, 5: 1911, 187-196.

*32. J. C. Bell. Recent literature on the Binet tests. *JEdPs*, 3: 1912, 101-110.

33. Binet and Simon. Le développement de l'intelligence chez les enfants. *AnPs*, 14: 1908, 1-94.

*34. A. Binet. Sur la nécessité d'une méthode applicable au diagnostic des arriérés militaires. *Annales med.-psych.*, Jan.-Feb., 1910.

35. A. Binet. La mesure du développement de l'intelligence chez les jeunes enfants. *Bull. de la soc. libre pour l'étude ps. de l'enfant*. Paris, 1911, Nos. 10 and 11, pp. 187-248.

36. Binet et Simon. Nouvelles recherches sur la mesure du niveau intellectuel chez les enfants d'école. *AnPs*, 17: 1911, 145-201.

*37. A. Binet. Die neuen Gedanken über das Schulkind. Bearb. v. G. Anschütz und W. J. Ruttmann. Leipzig, 1912. Pp. 289.

*38. E. Bloch und Anna Preiss. Ueber Intelligenzprüfung an normalen Volksschulkindern nach Bobertag (Methode Binet-Simon). *ZAngPs*, 6: 1912, 539-547. (Cf. notes at the end.)

39. O. Bobertag. Binets Arbeiten über die intellektuelle Entwicklung des Schulkindes. *ZAngPs*, 3: 1909, 230-259.

40. O. Bobertag. Ueber Intelligenzprüfung. I. Methodik und Ergebnisse der einzelnen Tests. *ZAngPs*, 5: 1911, 105-203. II. Gesamtergebnisse der Methode. *ZAngPs*, 6: 1912, 495-538. (Cf. notes at the end.)

*41. O. Bobertag. Intelligenzprüfungen an Schulkindern. *Die Grenzboten*, 70: 1911, 375-384.

*42. O. Bobertag. Quelques réflexions méthodologiques à propos de 'l'échelle metrique de Binet et Simon.' *AnPs*, 18: 1912, 271-288.

*43. F. Chotzen. Die Bedeutung der Intelligenzprüfungmethode von Binet-Simon f. d. Hilfsschule. *Die Hilfsschule*, 5: 1912, pp. 10.

*44. F. Chotzen. Die Intelligenzprüfungmethode von Binet-Simon bei schwachsinnigen Kindern. (Unter Mitwirkung von Dr. M. Nicolauer.) *ZAngPs*, 6: 1912, 411-494. (Cf. notes at the end.)

45. O. Decroly et J. Degand. La mesure de l'intelligence chez les enfants normaux d'apres les tests de MM. Binet et Simon. Nouvelle contribution critique. *ArdePs*, 9: 1910, 81-108.

*46. A. Descoeudres. Les tests de Binet et Simon et leur valeur scolaire. *ArdePs*, 11: 1911, 331-350.

47. H. H. Goddard. Four hundred feeble-minded children classified by the Binet method. *PdSe*, 17: 1910, 387-397.

48. H. H. Goddard. Two thousand normal children measured by the Binet measuring scale of intelligence. *PdSe*, 18: 1911, 232-259.

49. H. H. Goddard. Die Untersuchung d. Intellekts schwachsinniger Kinder. *Eos*, 6: 1909, 177-197.

*50. Clara H. Town. The Binet-Simon scale and the psychologist. *PsCl*, 5: 1912, 239-244.

*51. A. Jeronutti. *Rivista pedagogica*, 3: 1909, No. 3.

*52. Katherine L. Johnston. An English version of Binet's tests for the measurement of intelligence. *Training College Record*, Nov., 1910.

*53. E. A. Kirkpatrick. The Binet tests and mental ability. *JEdPs*, 3: 1912, 337.

54. F. Kramer. Die Intelligenzprüfung bei kriminellen und psychopathischen Kindern. Vortrag, 1911. (See Reference 11.)

*55. I. Lawrence. A study of the Binet definition tests. *PsCl*, 5: 1911, 207-216.

*56. I. B. MacDonald. The Binet tests in a hospital for the insane. *TrSc*, 7: 1910.

*57. M. Morlé. L'influence du milieu social sur le degré de l'intelligence des enfants. *Bull. de la soc. libre*, etc. 12: 1911, No. 1.

*58. Clara Schmitt. The Binet-Simon tests of mental ability. Discussion and criticism. *PdSe*, 19: 1912, 186-200.

*59. Anna Schubert. Versuch einer Anwendung d. System v. Binet an russische Kindern. Vortrag, S.-A. aus Bericht u. d. I. russ. Kong. f. exp. Päd. in St. Petersburg. Dec., 1910. Pp. 26. (In Russian.)

*60. H. Seifert. Alfred Binet und seine Intelligenzprüfung. *Kathol. Schulzeitung f. Norddeutschland*, 29 (9).

*61. F. C. Shrubsall. The examination of mentally defective children. *School Hygiene* (London), 2: 1911, No. 11.

62. W. Stern. Fragestellungen, Methoden und Ergebnisse der Intelligenzprüfung. (See Reference 11.)

*63. L. M. Terman. The Binet-Simon scale for measuring intelligence; Impressions gained by its application. *PsCl*, 5: 1911, 199-206.

*64. L. M. Terman and H. G. Childs. A tentative revision and extension of the Binet-Simon measuring scale of intelligence. *JEdPs*, 3: 1912, 61-74, 133-143, 198-208, 277-289.

*65. Z. Treves ed U. Saffiotti. La 'scala metrica dell' intelligenza' di Binet e Simon. Nota preventiva. Milan (*Laboratorio civico di Ps.*), 1910.

*66. Z. Treves ed U. Saffiotti. La 'scala metrica dell' intelligenza' di Binet e Simon. Studiata nelle Scuole communali elementari di Milano. Esposizione e critica. Milan (*Laboratorio civico di Ps. pura ed applicata*), 1911. Pp. 67.

*67. J. E. W. Wallin. A practical guide for the administration of the Binet-Simon scale for measuring intelligence. *PsCl*, 5: 1911, 217-238.

*68. J. E. W. Wallin. Human efficiency. *PdSe*, 18: 1911, 74-84.

*69. L. E. Widen. A comparison of the Binet and Simon method and two discrimination methods for measuring mental age. (Thesis.) Iowa City, 1911.

C. On Part III.

(Rank-order Method. Correlation. Teachers' Estimates.)

See also literature cited in Reference 1, pp. 391-392.

70. W. Betz. Ueber Korrelation. Methoden d. Korr. Berechnung u. krit. Bericht über Korr.—Untersuchungen a. d. Geb. d. Intelligenz, d. Anlagen u. ihre Beeinflussung durch äussere Umstände. *Beiheft zur ZAngPs* (3), 1911. Pp. 88.

*71. A. Binet. Comment les instituteurs jugent-ils l'intelligence d'un écolier? *Bull. de la soc. libre*, etc. 1910, p. 172.

72. C. Burt. Experimental tests of general intelligence. *BrJPs*, 3: 1909, 94-177.

*73. Alice Descoeudres. Exploration de quelques tests d'intelligence chez des enfants anormaux et arriérés. *ArdePs*, 11: 1911, 351-375.

*74. W. H. Gilby, assisted by K. Pearson. On the significance of the teacher's appreciation of general intelligence. *Biometrika*, 8: 1911, 94-108.

*75. B. Hart and C. Spearman. General ability, its existence and nature. *BrJPs*, 5: 1912, 51-79.

*76. H. Gertrude Jones. On the value of the teacher's opinion of the general intelligence of school children. *Biometrika*, 7: 1910, 542-548.

77. F. Krueger und C. Spearman. Die Korrelation zwischen verschiedenen geistigen Leistungsfähigkeiten. *ZPs*, 44: 1906, 50-114.

78. G. Ries. Beitrag zur Methodik der Intelligenzprüfung. *ZPs*, 56: 1910, 321-343.

79. C. Spearman. The proof and measurement of association between two things. *AmJPs*, 15: 1904, 72-101.

80. C. Spearman. 'General Intelligence' objectively determined and measured. *AmJPs*, 15: 1904, 201-292.

*81. H. Waite. The teacher's estimation of the general intelligence of school children. *Biometrika*, 8: 1911, 79-93.

Note: Heft 5/6 of *ZAngPs*, Vol. 6, which contains the articles of Bobertag (40, II), Chotzen (44) and Block u. Preiss (38), can also be purchased separately through book sellers.

APPENDICES

APPENDIX I.

Example of the Computation of a Correlation.

Correlation between 'class-place' (x) and a teacher's estimate of intelligence (y).

$$\text{Index of correlation} = \varrho = 1 - \frac{6\Sigma\,(x-y)^2}{n\,(n^2-1)}.$$

$$\text{Probable error} = P.\,E. = .706\,\frac{1-\varrho^2}{\sqrt{n}}.$$

($n = 23$ pupils in *Untertertia*—grade entered at about 12 years.)

Pupils	x	y	$x-y$	$(x-y)^2$
A	1	10	− 9	81
B	2	14	−12	144
C	3	13	−10	100
D	4	1	+ 3	9
E	5	5	0	0
F	6	7	− 1	1
G	7	20	−13	169
H	8	2	+ 6	36
I	9	8	+ 1	1
J	10	15	− 5	25
K	11	9	+ 2	4
L	12	22	−10	100
M	13	4	+ 9	81
N	14	11	+ 3	9
O	15	3	+12	144
P	16	21	− 5	25
Q	17	6	+11	121
R	18	18	0	0
S	19	12	+ 7	49
T	20	16	+ 4	16
U	21	23	− 2	4
V	22	17	+ 5	25
W	23	19	+ 4	16
			Sum	1160

$$\varrho = 1 - \frac{6\,.\,1160}{23\,(23^2-1)} = 0.43.$$

$$P.\,E. = 0.706\,\frac{1-0.43^2}{\sqrt{23}} = 0.12.$$

Appendix II. Arrangements of the Binet-Simon System.

Age-level.	*Binet-Simon System.* 1908 (33) | 1911 (35, 36) (Each age-level contains 5 tests.) (Asterisk denotes that the test is not used in the other system. A number following a test shows what year, if different, it occupies in the other system.)	Provisional Rearrangement by *Bobertag*, 1912 (40, II) The arrangement is intended to eliminate the excessive ease of the lower ages and the excessive difficulties of the upper ages. Each age-level between 5 and 10 contains 5 tests. The tests for 11 and 12 are combined, and here 3 successes count as one and six successes as two years. Up to the present the system has been used by Chotzen and Bobertag. The figures in parenthesis following the tests show the age-level (if different) occupied by the test in the 1908 Binet-Simon series. An asterisk denotes a new test.	*Terman and Childs* 1912 (64, pp. 277-281) Thirteen age-levels with some new tests. Some of the tests are repeated at several ages, but with varying requirements. The standards for grading these requirements are still wanting in some cases. The utility of the system has not yet been confirmed by further testing, so that the arrangement is to be considered only as a proposed system.	Age-level.
3	Points to mouth eye and nose. Repeats 6-syllabled sentences. Repeats 2 digits. Enumerates parts of pictures. Knows family name.		Naming key, knife and coin. Enumeration of parts of picture. Repeats 3 digits. Knows sex. Comparison of two weights. "What's the thing to do when you feel sleepy (cold) ?"	3
4	Names objects shown. Repeats 3 digits. Knows sex. Compares 2 lines (5 and 6 cm.)		Counts four pennies. Divided rectangle. Copies square. Esthetic comparison. Defines concrete objects by use.	4
5	Repeats 10-syllabled sentences. Counts four pennies. Copies square. Comparison of two weights (3 and 12 g.) Divided rectangle.	Repeats 10-syllabled sentences. Counts 4 pennies. Copies square. Defines concrete objects by use (6). Repeats 4 digits.*	Tells morning from afternoon. Names four chief colors. Executes triple command. Repeats 13-syllabled sentence. Vocabulary index : score?	5

6	Esthetic comparison. Tells morning from afternoon. Defines concrete objects by use. Executes triple command (7). Repeats 16-syllabled sentences.* Knows right hand and left ear (7).	Copies diamond (7). Counts 13 pennies (7).	Esthetic comparison. Executes triple command. Repeats 16-syllabled sentences. Divided rectangle (5). Describes picture (7).	Knows right hand and left ear. Knows number of fingers. Counts 13 pennies. Repeats 4 digits. Solves 3 easy problem-questions. Vocabulary index 12%.	6
7	Describes pictures. Repeats 5 digits (8). Copies diamond (6). Counts 13 pennies (6). Knows number of fingers.* Copies "The little Paul."* Knows coins from sou to franc.* Recognizes omissions in drawings (8).	Executes triple command (6). Knows right hand and left ear (6). Adds 3 single and 3 double sous (8). Names four chief colors (8).	Repeats 5 digits. Copies diamond. Knows coins from 1 Pf. to 1 Mk. Recognizes omissions in drawings. Knows right hand and left ear (6).	Describes pictures. Copies diamond. Names 4 coins. Recognizes omissions in drawings. Repeats 14 16-syllabled sentences. Vocabulary index 14%.	7
8	Counts from 20 to 1. Compares 2 objects from memory. Writes from dictation: "The sun shines."* Adds 3 single and 3 double sous (7). Names four chief colors (7). Recalls 2 items in passage read.*	Repeats 5 digits (7). Recognizes omissions in drawings (7). Names date (9).	Counts from 20 to 1. Compares two objects from memory. Names 4 chief colors. Solves 3 easy problem-questions (10). Reports one important point in a newspaper paragraph just heard.*	Counts from 20 to 1. Compares two objects from memory. Writes from dictation: "The pretty little girl." Repeats 5 digits. Vocabulary index 18%. Ball and field. (A circle is drawn to represent a field in which a ball is lost. Draw the best way to go to be sure to find the ball.)	8
9	Definitions superior to use. Makes change for 80 centimes from 1 fr. Recalls 6 items in passage read.* Recites days of the week.* Names date (8). Arranges 5 weights (10).	Recites months (10). Knows all coins (10). Solves 3 easy problem-questions (10).	Defines by superordinates. Makes change for 80 Pf. from 1 Mk. Explains pictures when helped by questions.* Names date. Arranges 5 weights.	Names date. Arranges 5 weights. Recalls 4 items in passage read. Gives total cost of 3 1-cent and 3 2-cent stamps. Names 50 words in 2 minutes. Solves 3 hard problem-questions. Vocabulary index 23%. Completion test; score?	9
10	Makes 2 sentences to include 3 words. Solves 5 hard problem-questions. Recites months (9). Knows all coins (9). Solves 3 easy problem-questions (9).	Arranges 5 weights (9). Criticizes 'absurdities' (11). Copies drawings from memory.	Makes 2 sentences to include 3 words. Knows all German coins. Reports 6 points in newspaper paragraph (9). Repeats 26-syllabled sentence (12). Repeats 6 digits.*	Makes sentence to include 3 words. Repeats 5 digits. Makes change for 4c. from a quarter. Vocabulary index 26%. Completion test: score 20. Ball and field: score 3. Interprets fables.	10

APPENDIX II. ARRANGEMENTS OF THE BINET-SIMON SYSTEM.—(Continued.)

Age-level.	*Binet-Simon System.*		Provisional Rearrangement by *Bobertag,* 1912 (40, II)	*Terman and Childs* 1912 (64, pp. 277-281)	Age-level.
11	Makes one sentence to include 3 words (12). Defines abstract terms (12). Rearranges sentences (12). Names 60 words in 3 minutes (12). Criticizes 'absurdities' (10).		Makes 1 sentence to include 3 words (11). Defines abstract terms (11). Rearranges sentences (11). Criticizes 'absurdities' (11). Explains pictures spontaneously (12). Makes 3 rimes in 1 minute (12). Completion test (12). Solves hard problem-questions (10).	Solves 5 arithmetical problems. Solves 4 hard problem-questions. Completion test: score 25. Vocabulary index 30%. Interprets fables. Sees points of 5 jokes.	11
12	Explains pictures (15). Repeats 7 digits (15). Repeats 26-syllabled sentences (15). Makes 3 rimes in 1 minute (15). Completion test (15).	Makes one sentence to include 3 words (11). Defines abstract terms (11). Rearranges sentences (11). Names 60 words in 3 min. (11). Resists line suggestion.*		Rearranges sentences. Notes 4 of 5 'absurdities.' Recalls 7 items in passage read. Repeats 26-syllabled sentence. Resist line-suggestion. Vocabulary index 36%.	12
13	Cut and folded paper test (adult). Juxtaposed triangles (adult). Distinguishes abstract terms (adult).			Repeats 7 digits. Interprets fables. Arithmetical reasoning: score? Vocabulary index 42%. Completion test: score 36. Solves 'problems of fact.'	13
15		Explains pictures (12). Repeats 7 digits (12). Repeats 26-syllabled sentence (12). Makes 3 rimes in 1 min. (12). Completion test (12).		Reverses clock-hands. Interprets fables: score? Interprets pictures. Vocabulary index: score? Completion test: score? Code test.	15
Adult.		Cut and folded paper test (13). Juxtaposed triangles (13). Distinguishes abstract terms (13). Distinguishes king and president.* Gives sense of selection.*		Reversed triangle. Distinguishes president and king. Ball and field: score 4. Completion test: score ? Gives sense of selection (Binet, 1911).	Adult.

INDEX